# INSTANT REFERRALS

## BRADLEY J. SUGARS

**McGraw-Hill**

New York   Chicago   San Francisco   Lisbon   London
Madrid   Mexico City   Milan   New Delhi   San Juan
Seoul   Singapore   Sydney   Toronto

The *McGraw·Hill* Companies

Dedicated to all *Action* Business Coaches,
leaders in every sense of the word

1 2 3 4 5 6 7 8 9 0    FGR/FGR    0 9 8 7 6 5

ISBN 0-07-146667-3

This publication is designed to provide accurate and authoritative information in regard to the subject matter covered. It is sold with the understanding that neither the author nor the publisher is engaged in rendering legal, accounting, or other professional service. If legal advice or other expert assistance is required, the services of a competent professional person should be sought.
—From a Declaration of Principles jointly adopted by Committee of the American Bar Association and a Committee of Publishers.

McGraw-Hill books are available at special quantity discounts to use as premiums and sales promotions, or for use in corporate training programs. For more information, please write to the Director of Special Sales, McGraw-Hill Professional, Two Penn Plaza, New York, NY 10121-2298. Or contact your local bookstore.

Library of Congress Cataloging-in-Publication Data

Sugars, Bradley J.
  Instant referrals / Bradley J. Sugars.
  p.   cm.
  Includes bibliographical references.
  ISBN 0-07-146667-3 (pbk. : alk. paper)
  1. Relationship marketing.   2. Business referrals.
  3. Marketing—Management.   I. Title.
    HF5415.55.S34 2006
    658.8—dc22                                    2005054503

# INSTANT REFERRALS

**Action International**
**Business Coaching**

# ∎ CONTENTS

# ▌ INTRODUCTION

One of the most fundamental functions of any business is to ensure that it has a constant supply of new leads to attempt to do business with. And it really doesn't matter what type of business you run; you simply need someone to do business with. Otherwise you can't claim to be in business.

Chasing new leads is thought of by many as something of a specialty area, yet it needn't be. It is really quite simple and straightforward once you know how.

How many people do you know who will tell you that they hate cold calling? I'm sure the answer will be many. Yet some people thrive on it. Some people love the challenge of confronting complete strangers and trying to do business with them when they, the other parties, haven't initiated the meeting. But most don't, so let's consider this in a little more detail. Let's consider the situation where our hypothetical salesperson is like most and doesn't particularly like cold calling as a means of finding leads for his business.

The situation would be quite different if these two people were to meet under different circumstances, wouldn't it? For instance, if the would-be customer were to approach the salesperson because of a need for a product the salesperson happened to be selling, how would the salesperson handle the encounter this time? Very differently, because for a start, the salesperson would typically be on home territory and in control of the situation.

Yet why should that same salesperson handle things differently in these two hypothetical situations?

When you really think about it, it all comes down to whether or not our hypothetical salesperson is operating within or outside her comfort zone.

You see, you just have to ask those who cold call regularly and they will tell you they didn't like it at first, but once they began doing it regularly, they got used to it and their results improved. It could be argued that their results improved because they became better at it, but I won't push this point of view here. The important point is that there came a time when cold calling became part of their comfort zone—they became comfortable doing business this way.

Real estate agents, insurance agents, commission salespeople, and a host of others rely on cold-calling strategies and with practice they find they lose their fear for walking up to someone's front door, knocking, and striking up a conversation.

Where is this leading us? Well, apart from the fear factor, cold calling is also an expensive way of sourcing leads. It's not only expensive in terms of the cost of physically getting to the area you want to work, but also it's expensive in terms of labor, time, and mental energy.

Now while cold calling is an important strategy for finding leads, it's obviously not the only one. There is a whole range of strategies every business should be using. You can read more about this in my book *Instant Leads*. These include things like classified advertising, radio campaigns, the Yellow Pages, establishing host-beneficiary relationships and strategic alliances, and developing a unique selling proposition.

But perhaps one of the best and most exciting ways of getting new leads for your business is through referrals. You see, it's very powerful when someone says to a friend, "You've got to buy from them because they are simply the best."

This book is all about building a referral-based business. It will tell you everything you need to know about how to go about building a business that will build itself. It will tell you why this is the best type of business you could possibly want and how you can go about delivering the *wow* factor to your customers time and time again.

This book is all about turning your existing customers into Raving Fans who will insist that their family and friends become Raving Fans too.

This book will help rev up your business in the most cost-effective way possible by getting your existing customers to promote your business for you.

# ■ HOW TO USE THIS BOOK

This book is designed to be a workbook that will help you build a referral-based business, so use it as such. It contains details of 21 powerful strategies you can use to get your business revving on all cylinders.

These strategies will not only transform your business; they will also transform the way you go about business. The second part of this statement is significant, because you need to bear in mind that *you* need to *do* things to transform your business. You see, if you don't take *Action* yourself, then you'll continue to get the same results from your business that you are currently getting. If you've always baked chocolate cakes and now want to bake an apple pie, you need to use a different recipe because you need to do things differently. If you don't, guess what you'll end up with. A chocolate cake.

*Action* is the operative word here. That's why this is an *Action* book. It involves your reading, then doing a whole lot of things. These could range from thinking and planning to testing and measuring, writing, and implementing strategies.

So make notes as you go along. They will come in handy later on when the time comes to implement the strategies. You will also read about my friend Charlie, who successfully transformed his garage into a referral-based business. Follow his exploits as he implemented the various strategies mentioned in this book. And while on the subject of strategies, you can implement them one at a time or in groups. Some may be more appealing to your business than others, but they will all work. You may even be using some of them already. If you are, that's fantastic. But if you aren't, then what are you waiting for? There is more referral business out there waiting for you.

There's never been a better time to get into action than now, so let's get right into it, shall we?

Part 1

# ▪ Understand What a Referral-Based Business Is

Charlie had always been keen on the idea of sitting back and waiting for customers to call and book their cars in for service. And in this respect he is no different than the vast majority of car-servicing businesses. You see, his training is in the field of motor mechanics and not business or marketing.

But as we all know, the world doesn't work like that, but it can, if you put in place certain strategies.

I remember Charlie becoming very excited when I first mentioned this possibility to him. He said that, while this was the ideal business model he dreamed about, he didn't think it was something that could work, even if it were feasible. He also said that he had never heard of a business that operated that way before.

Imagine his surprise when I told him it was not only a realistic possibility; it was also very easy to achieve.

"What you want is a referral-based business, Charlie," I said. "But before you dive in and begin changing the way you do business, you need to have a clear understanding of just what a referral-based business is."

"Why's that, Brad? I mean, I love the sound of a business in which I don't have to do all that marketing stuff—I dream about having customers showing up out of the blue and wanting me to service their cars. This, I know, is the ideal business because I am not really a marketing type. I'm not comfortable doing all that stuff. Give me a set of spanners rather than a computer and telephone any day."

I knew exactly what he meant. I had come across this comment countless times before.

"Charlie, you still need to do a certain amount of marketing. It's just that in this type of business, you go about it in a different way. There may be a lot less marketing to do, but you still do need to market your business. The real difference is that the leads you get are more qualified and your emphasis will be on sourcing customers who will be with you for a long time. This in itself will mean the type of marketing, as well as the amount you do, will be radically different than that done by normal businesses. But before we get into that, let's discuss what a referral-based business actually is.

He agreed, so I pressed on.

"Well, as the name implies, a referral-based business is one that relies largely on referral strategies to generate business.

"A business doesn't have to always have been set up to run on referrals; it can be changed to become a referral-based business at any stage."

So if you, the reader, already have a business and would like to alter the way you go about your business by tapping into your existing customer base more, then read on. It's never too late.

"Before we look now at various referral strategies, let's first consider what a referral strategy is," I continued.

He nodded.

"A referral strategy is simply a way of introducing new customers to your business for a low acquisition cost. Basically, it's a way of getting your existing customers to promote your business for you. It's a way of getting them to introduce their family, friends, and colleagues to your product or service."

"Hang on, Brad," Charlie interjected. "What does an acquisition cost have to do with it? For that matter, what exactly is an acquisition cost?"

Here we'll leave Charlie for the time being as we take a closer look at some of the concepts involved with business in general.

## Acquisition Cost

Imagine having to work out how much your business should spend on sales and marketing. Setting a budget this way is as hard as finding a needle in a haystack.

Let me show you how you can have an unlimited marketing budget, and buy—that's right, *buy*—as many customers as you want. It's like turning on the tap to business profits.

Instead of spending a fixed amount on sales and marketing, when you take on the idea of investing in sales and marketing you've got to understand that every investment has a purchase price. In business most people think that you just invest in the stock you sell—but the same is also true of customers.

In fact, from a marketing point of view, the only thing you've got to buy are new customers. The question really is, how much are you paying for them?

If you put $1000 into advertising and this generates 100 phone calls, then you're paying $10 for each lead. Then if you only sell to one in five of those leads, you're paying $50 (5 × $10) for each sale.

Let's look at another example. A clothing store regularly runs an ad in the local newspaper. It's the only ad they run, so testing and measuring its effectiveness is straightforward. The ad costs them $370 a week and it generates, on average, 25 inquiries. The owner is understandably delighted because he understands that he is paying $14.80 per inquiry. And he knows that he couldn't get them cheaper. And to make this marketing strategy even more attractive, he also knows that closing sales is his strong point. Of the 25 prospects that come in every week, 19 leave with a purchase. His conversion rate is 76 percent. The net result of his marketing campaign is that each new customer costs him $19.47.

Now, here's where this all gets exciting.

Going back to the first example above, imagine that you were a business owner who was about to develop a new marketing plan. Let's say your business was a camera shop. Now you already know that each new customer costs you $50. Let's assume now that you also know, from analyzing your sales records, that each customer spends, on average, $500. This means your average dollar sale is $500. Your records also show that your average profit margin is $100.

What does all this tell you? It tells you that for every $50 you invest you make $100.

The next question you need to ask yourself is this: How many times could you invest that $50?

The answer is as many times as you want, because every time you spent $50, you'd make $100. That would be a good deal, wouldn't it? You bet it would.

It almost sounds too good to be true, doesn't it? But it really is as simple as that! Once you know how much it costs to buy a customer, and as long as you make more per customer than the acquisition cost, you're ready to start reaping the profits.

OK, so let's look some more into this notion of "buying" a customer.

## Buying a Customer

What's the difference between buying a customer and what you're doing at present in your business? That's the difference between selling to a customer and buying one.

The difference is huge.

When you switch from selling to new customers to focusing on buying new ones, you'll start to see a whole new and unlimited world of sales and marketing results.

Try to see the entire function of your business as nothing more than a buying exercise—an exercise of buying customers, *not* selling products or services. Then the only real question you've got to ask is this: can you buy customers for less than you'll profit from them over their lifetime of buying?

As soon as you start to see your business as a total marketing entity and *not* a production, service, or retail entity, you'll understand why the price you pay for customers is your biggest expense.

But here is something even more powerful. What if you could buy them for less than your profits on your first sale, and what if that first sale came within days of the commencement of your marketing campaign?

It's around this time in the learning cycle that people start getting really excited. And it's only the beginning because when we start getting customers to keep coming back and spending more per visit, that's when real wealth starts accumulating.

There's one more concept I want to explain at this stage. It's the lifetime value of a customer, and something I referred to earlier.

## Lifetime Value

Think about this for a moment. How much are you going to spend in your lifetime on something as simple as toilet paper? Thousands of dollars?

So let me ask you this. How much will the average customers in your business spend with you over their lifetimes?

Let me give you an example. In my dog food business, I knew the average person would spend $800 a year on her dog, and the average dog lives for 10 years. So, assuming a customer only stays with me for half of that time—five years—then she is worth $4000 to me.

Then, what if she refers to me two new customers in the first year. Now the original customer is worth three times $4000—or $12,000.

What if she also then referred another two every year, and every referral sent us another two customers a year? How much is she now worth to me now? Hundreds of thousands?

Now more to the point; how much are your customers worth to you over their lifetimes of buying from you?

You must establish this long-term view of their value firmly in your mind before you can appreciate how important it is to develop a relationship with customers and to ensure everything is done to keep them for as long as possible.

## The Difference between a Promotion and a Business

This raises an amazingly powerful business point. What's the difference between a promotion and a business?

Many business owners have just a promotion and go through life thinking they have a business. Confused? Let me explain.

With a promotion, you have one product, one service, and once you've sold it to someone, that's it. You've got to go out and find yourself another customer. So what you have is an ongoing marketing promotion, *not* a business.

On the other hand, a business is where you buy customers and then sell something or many things to them over and over and over again.

By the way, who ever said you can't sell someone else's products or services and get paid a commission for the referral? This happens all the time and it's very profitable business. Are you missing out?

Strategic alliances with other businesses can be a very powerful way to increase your customer base for a relatively low outlay. And, what's more, by linking up with the right businesses, you can target the exact type of customer who offers the best return on your acquisition cost.

## What Makes a Successful Referral Strategy?

At this point it's important to consider just what makes a strategy successful. You see, it's pointless to have a strategy in place if it doesn't contribute to your bottom line.

There are a number of elements which, when combined, make a referral strategy successful. These range from finding the right type of customer to the strategy that best suits your type of business. But there are two things you need to understand above all else:

### Service

Your service must be extraordinary. Having good or even great service just won't do. If you want people to refer their friends, then make sure your service is first-rate. How do your customers really feel about doing business with you?

The first thing you need to understand is that customers *expect* to be satisfied when making contact with any business. They have a need they want satisfied. They've also gone to the trouble of finding out which businesses can satisfy that need; then they've done something about it—they've either phoned or actually traveled to your business. What happens next will determine the lasting impression they have of your business.

They *expect* satisfaction, but will actually talk to others about your business if they get more than they *expect*.

So give them something to talk about.

This is the first step to creating a Raving Fan.

Good customer service is proactive. Don't wait until you have a problem in this area before doing something about it—before you think about ways and means of taking care of your customers. How can you give your customers something more than they expect?

Think of different things you could do to get them talking. Brainstorm. Consult your salespeople. Start becoming innovative in this area. Think outside the box.

Make this part of your routine. Get used to constantly searching for new ways of satisfying your customers. Keep your eyes open, watch what other businesses are doing, and keep innovating. You see, customers actually *expect* you to keep getting better.

So what actually are Raving Fans? Raving Fans are people who can't stop selling for you. They do this, of course, by continually referring people to you. The exciting thing about Raving Fans is they can almost be regarded as part of your team. They want to see you succeed. Of course, they continue buying from you all along.

## Your Offer

If you don't give people a good reason, a "what's in it for me?," your strategy will fail. Some of the strategies you'll discover in this book will rely on your offer more heavily than others, but regardless of which ones you choose, always ask yourself this: "Would I refer someone for that reason?"

In the following pages you'll learn how to put a referral strategy into place, which type suits which businesses, the types of customers you want referred to you, and just as importantly, those you would rather not have.

**Part 2**

# ▮ Is a Referral-Based Business for You?

"Before deciding which referral strategies to implement first, Charlie, you need to work out whether this is the right overall approach for you and your business," I explained, not wanting to get Charlie's hopes up unnecessarily. I wanted him to give this careful consideration because it does require a certain level of commitment.

"You need to consider whether adopting a referral-based business model is the correct one for your business," I continued. He didn't object, so I pushed on.

"To help you arrive at a considered decision, you need to compare the potential returns you will get if your business were structured along referral lines to that which it is currently getting, based on more traditional lines. You need to take a close look at the marketing implications of the two approaches."

He now had something to say, and I let him.

"So, how do you do that? And what exactly is the difference between them anyway?"

"While a business that is geared predominantly towards referral strategies typically has a low hard-dollar cost, some referral strategies can nevertheless be quite time-consuming."

"A referral approach is ideal for a business that stocks, provides, or sells a higher-priced product or service—just like you do, Charlie," I continued.

"Whereas almost any type of business can benefit from having a referral strategy (or a number of them for that matter), there are some businesses it doesn't suit quite as well. For example, it's probably inappropriate for a fast food outlet, as these businesses tend to have too many customers at any one time anyway. They would gain very little from having more referred."

I paused to let that sink in. Then I went on.

"Having said that, a strategy where your customers could take a card or a flyer and pass it on to their friends could work quite well in that business. You could also have an offer for groups of four or more. In that business you want to use the right low-cost referral strategy."

Charlie was nodding away to himself as I spoke. This was a sure sign it was making sense to him.

"What you really need to do first and foremost is to understand what your actual costs are. Do you know how many leads you get each month? Do you know what your conversion rate is? This means how many leads are converted into customers when they actually do business with you. And what about the average number of transactions each customer makes? Do you know this number? Of course, you should know the average dollar sale price of your merchandise. And what about your margins? Do you know the percentage of each sale that's profit? These are all vital pieces of information that every business owner needs to know. How about you, Charlie? Can you list these figures? If not, read my book *Instant Cashflow* to find out how you can measure them."

At this point it's time to leave Charlie for a while and turn our attention to *your* business. This is where you get to *do* something.

Do you have a reasonable idea of what those numbers are? If so, it's time to fill in the chart on page 14. If not, take some time now to find out what they are (even if it's only a best-guess) so you can fill in the chart.

Let's work through it one step at a time.

## Leads

This is the total number of potential buyers that you contacted or that contacted you last year. Also known as prospects, or potentials. Most businesspeople confuse responses, or the number of potential buyers, with results. Just because the phone is ringing doesn't mean the cash register is. And what's even more amazing is that very few businesses even know how many leads they get a week, let alone from each and every marketing campaign. It's great to get a lot of leads, but then you've got to remember your conversion rate.

## Conversion Rate

This is the percentage of people who did buy versus those who could have bought. For example, if you had 10 people walk through your store today and you sold to only 3 of them, you'd have a conversion rate of 3 out of 10, or 30 percent. This has to be a literal gold mine in almost every business I walk into. You've already got them interested; now you've just got to get them over the line. When I ask average business owners about their conversion rate, they take a stab in the dark and tell me that it's between 60 and 70 percent. Just for fun, I get them to measure it, and a couple of weeks later we find that it is more like 20 or 30 percent. Imagine how you'd feel if this were you.

You should feel great! In fact you should be excited, because if you were getting by at 20 or 30 percent, imagine how your business would run at 60 or 70 percent. Remember, double your conversion rate and you've just doubled your turnover.

## Your Number of Customers

This is the number of different customers you deal with. You work it out by multiplying the total number of leads by the conversion rate. I'll run through an example in just a moment. Remember, *it's not about getting more customers;* you can't change that. It's about getting more leads and then improving your conversion rate. These are the variables that lead to the result.

## Your Number of Transactions

This is another of the five main variables of what I call the Business Chassis. Some of your customers will buy from you weekly, others monthly, others on the odd occasion, and others just once in their lifetimes. What you want to know now is the average. Not your best and not your worst, but the average number of times one of your customers buys from you in a year. Once again, here's another gold mine; most businesspeople never collect a database of their past customers, let alone write to them or call them and ask them to come back.

## Your Average Dollar Sale

Here's one variable that at least some business owners do measure. Once again, some customers might spend $5000 and some just $5, but the average is what you're after. To work it out, add up your total sales and divide this number by your number of sales.

## Your Revenues

This is another result. You'll see what I mean by this in a minute. Multiply the total number of customers you dealt with by the number of times they came back on average, and then by the average amount they spent with you each time. That's your turnover. Put simply, Customers × Transactions × Average $ Sale = Revenues. See, revenues is a result because it comes after the equals sign in the above formula. This is another area most business owners will know the answer to. Yet they most probably have no real idea how they got to it. Of course, you want more of it, but *you can't get more revenues.* What you can get is more transactions, and a higher average dollar sale with the total number of customers you deal with.

## Your Margins

This is the percentage of each and every sale that's profit. In other words, if you sold something for $100 and $25 was profit, then you've got a 25 percent margin. Remember, this is after all costs are taken out. It's potentially another little gold mine for you to tap into.

## Your Profits

Here we have another result that every business owner wants more of, not realizing that *you can't get more profit,* but what you can get is get greater margins on the turnover you've got. And that's it.

The Business Chassis I've outlined above is the basic model that dictates the profit levels of every business on earth.

By simply breaking down your business and marketing efforts (*selling is married to marketing*) into these five areas and understanding how each affects the other, you're halfway there—and way ahead of 90 percent of businesses out there.

## Now Let's Try It with a Few Numbers

To bring all of this home to you, let's put in some numbers that should help you make sense of it all.

| | | |
|---|---|---|
| **Leads** | 4000 | *(total from last year)* |
| | × | |
| **Conversion Rate** | 25% | *(you sold to 1 in 4)* |
| | = | |
| Customers | — | |
| | × | |
| **Transactions** | 2 | *(on average)* |
| | × | |
| **Average $ Sale** | $100 | *(on average)* |
| | = | |
| Revenues | — | |
| | × | |
| **Margins** | 25% | *(on average)* |
| | = | |
| Profit | — | |

So what does it all calculate out to?

| | | |
|---|---|---|
| **Leads** | 4000 | *(total from last year)* |
| | × | |
| **Conversion Rate** | 25% | *(you sold to 1 in 4)* |
| | = | |
| Customers | 1,000 | *(calculated out)* |
| | × | |
| **Transactions** | 2 | *(on average)* |
| | × | |
| **Average $ Sale** | $100 | *(on average)* |
| | = | |
| Revenues | $200,000 | *(calculated out)* |
| | × | |
| **Margins** | 25% | *(on average)* |
| | = | |
| Profit | $50,000 | *(calculated out)* |

Did you follow that? It's all pretty straightforward. Now it's time to put in some real numbers—yours.

Ready? OK, fill in the chart below.

LEADS: _____
(prospects or potential customers)

×

CONVERSION RATE: _____
(the difference between those that could have bought and those that did)

×

CUSTOMERS: _____
(the number of different customers you deal with)

×

NUMBER OF TRANSACTIONS: _____
(the average number of times each customer bought from you that year)

×

AVERAGE DOLLAR SALE PRICE: _____
(the average price of the items you sell)

=

TOTAL REVENUES: _____
(the total revenue of the business)

×

MARGINS: _____
(the percentage of each sale that's profit)

=

PROFIT: _____
(something every business owner wants more of)

Once you've completed the above exercise, you'll have a very good idea of precisely what it costs you to buy each customer you have. It may also be the very first time you've known these important figures. If this is the case, don't be alarmed because the vast majority of business owners are in the same position. You'd be surprised at how few actually have any idea what their conversion rate is.

Now that you have a good handle on these figures (or at least on what figures you need to work out over the next week or two), you have some choices. You could, for instance, choose to accept them and carry on as before, or you could choose to implement strategies that are more cost-effective and yield better results at the same time. It is my experience that there are few strategies that can outperform referral-based strategies.

## Part 3

# ▌ Get Clear on Who Your Target Market Is

It was now time to raise another important question with Charlie.

"Before you go down the route that will lead to the establishment of a referral-based business, the next thing you need to do is to decide on the type of customers you want to do business with, Charlie," I said.

"Why is that, Brad?" he asked.

"Simple. It's because the last thing in the world you want is to get referrals who don't translate into business. You know, the ones who only do business with you once and never return, or even worse, those who create more headaches than they do sales, and never give you the business you're really after."

"I'm with you, Brad. But how do you control who comes along wanting to have their car serviced here?"

"If you don't set the rules at the outset, your new customers will set them for you. So you need to decide who your ideal customer is. You need to form a mental picture of what your ideal customer looks like, where he lives, what he does for a living, and how much he earns. This is important because it's a simple fact that some customers are more trouble than they're worth. They will actually cost you money in the long run."

Here are the main guidelines to help you gain a clearer picture of your target market:

## Age

How old are they? Don't just say "all ages" or "a variety." We want to create a picture in your mind of your average customer. Think of an age that symbolizes most of them.

## Sex

Are they male or female? "Half and half" is too broad. Practically every business is split one way or the other. Give it some real thought. Which gender spends more with you or visits more often?

## Income

How much do they earn? Do they make a great living, meaning quality is the big issue, or are they scraping for every dollar, always looking for a deal? It's essential you find this out.

## Where Do They Live?

Are they local, or do they come from miles around to deal with you? This will dictate how you communicate with them.

## Who Is Your Ideal Customer?

It's often said there are customers, and there are customers. How true this is.

There are those customers you'd love to deal with every day, and there are those you'd wish never came back. But there are more than just two basic groups. There are, in fact, four categories, A, B, C and D. I explain them as follows:

**A**wesome

**B**asic

**C**an't deal with

**D**ead

What do these customers typically look like? How would you recognize them if they came into your business?

A-grade customers will usually spend more money and be less hassle than the others. B-grade customers are good, solid customers who may well be the lifeblood of the average business. They are more price conscious but not to the point of being a nuisance. C-grade customers demand a lot of your time, haggle on price, and take ages to make up their minds. D-grade customers are every business owner's worst nightmare. They always pay their accounts late, they make frequent returns, and they take up heaps of your time. They also frequently make "scenes" in the store if things don't pan out their way. They simply aren't worth having as customers.

You might wish to deal only with the A's and B's. If that's the case, get rid of the rest. How do you do that? Simple. Tell them. Or set up rules for doing business, then write to everyone on your database, explaining you're repositioning your business and here are the new rules. You can also change your pricing policy or the décor of your premises—this alone will filter out those you don't want. A video store wanted to shake off the young hooligans who had taken to gathering there. All they did was to change the type of music they played in the store. Instead of playing music teenagers listen to, they began playing classical music. Their client base changed virtually overnight.

If you were to really analyze your business, you'd find that 20 percent of your customers account for 80 percent of your business. This is what I call, the 80-20 Rule. Do you know who your 20 percent is? These are the ones you should be concentrating your efforts on.

## Part 4

# ▪ Know Exactly What You Are Offering

I'm not talking about the strategies here; those come later and in detail. I'm talking about the overall approach you are offering customers once you've decided that the referral-based business is the way to go.

I'm talking about what you're offering your target market or ideal customers.

"The first thing you need to do is to educate your customers, Charlie," I said.

"You need to let them know how to do business with you, what you expect of them as customers, and what they can expect in return. This may surprise you, because I'm sure you, like most business owners, probably believe that the customer comes first. This has got to be one of business's biggest myths."

He looked stunned. Speechless. Unable to say anything. So I continued.

"Let me explain what I mean."

"Every business has four categories of customer. They are, in order of importance:

1. The owner

2. The team

3. The suppliers

4. The customers

"The first three are vitally important, and together they aim at working well together so that they can collectively satisfy the customer or end user."

"Your business has to be built to serve *you* first and foremost with profit and enjoyment. Why else would you have established it in the first place?"

"I needed a job, Brad. Isn't that why most people start their own businesses?"

"Absolutely not, Charlie! Your business must serve you because you are the one, after all, who is taking all the risks and assuming ultimate responsibility."

I could tell, from the look in his eyes, that what I was saying suddenly made sense.

It was now time to consider his team.

"Without your team you have no business," I said.

"They are the ones that make it all happen for you, aren't they? I mean, you simply can't do it all yourself, can you? How could you possibly do all the book work, the marketing, answering the phone, ordering stock, and paying the bills while trying to work on all the cars that come in? The simple answer is you can't. To find out more about how to ensure your team is a dream team, read my book *Instant Team Building*."

I knew I wasn't telling him anything he didn't already know.

"Then there are your suppliers. Again, without them you'd most probably not be able to service any cars. You'd have no oil, spark plugs, or parts to use. Your reputation ultimately depends on theirs, because if you keep getting returns from your customers due to bad workmanship or inferior quality, your business will suffer."

He nodded in agreement.

"And here's another thing to consider; do you think it right that you should have to put up with third-rate customers who give you a hard time? Should you have to put up with being abused, shouted at, and made to look like an idiot just because that person is a customer? Of course not. As far as I'm concerned, that type of person can take her money and go elsewhere. I don't need her in my life or my business."

I could tell by his body language that he knew exactly what I was talking about here. Everyone who's been in business for a while will have come across this type of customer.

"You may not be able to choose your family, but you sure can choose whom you do business with.

"Understand that business is a cyclical phenomenon: As the owner of the business, if you look after your team, they will in turn look after the customers, who will in turn look after your business, which will then look after you. It's that simple.

"Every time you educate customers about how to go about doing business with you, you've got an advocate for life—with one condition: that you always give them the level of service you've promised. It doesn't have to be five-star service either, just the level of service you've promised. But it must be first-rate at whatever level you've promised."

"Here's another quick tip on educating people about doing business with you: be sure to let them know you're after quality people just like them. You'll be giving them a huge compliment and setting a standard for whom they refer to you right away."

Let's leave Charlie for a while and go back a step to discuss in more detail the notion of a customer becoming an advocate for life. I call these customers raving fans.

## Raving Fans

Raving Fans don't just happen. You have to work hard to get them there. How do you do that? I like to explain this using the *loyalty ladder* concept.

What I mean by this is you have to move your customers up this customer service ladder, and you need to keep them moving up all the time. So what is this loyalty ladder? Think of it just like an ordinary ladder.

If you were to step up onto the first rung of the ladder, would you just hang around there for a while before doing something? No, you would want to either continue climbing up right away, or you'd want to get off.

Now, ask yourself why it is you want to build a loyalty ladder for your business. I'd suggest it is because the first sale you make to a customer is made at a loss. Yes, statistics show 9 out of 10 first sales are made at a loss, because there are advertising costs, marketing costs, and commissions that first need to be taken into account. If you don't get that customer to come back and buy again, that customer isn't profitable to you.

Let's now take a closer look at the loyalty ladder and what the various stages on it involve:

## Suspect

When people first start out on the loyalty ladder, right at the bottom rung, they are called suspects. How do you identify them? They are only potential customers at this stage; they fit within your target market and they are willing to buy from you if they are in your geographic area.

## Prospect

We then move up the ladder to prospect. Prospects are suspects who have taken some sort of action like calling in response to an ad or visiting your business. You must collect all their details at this point so you can stay in touch with them. This is most important, as building customer loyalty is all about relationship building. You are aiming to build a database of prospects. Once you have done this, you will now use all your sales skills to move your prospects one rung up the ladder to the next stage, to that of customers.

## Shopper

Prospects become shoppers as soon as they have made one purchase. Here's something you'll find interesting: I find most businesses put up a huge stop sign at this level. The salespeople seem to sit back waiting for these customers to return, instead of being proactive and inviting them back. Understand that at this level, your customers have cost you money. If you are content to stop at this level, your business will eventually go broke. I have eaten at many restaurants, and guess what? I'm not on any database. I've never received a letter from any of them saying, "Brad, we'd love to have you back." This is, to my mind, quite insane. They seem to be saying, "You've bought, now I'm going to just hope like heck you come back and buy again, and again, and again." Think about the possibilities for your business. The stop sign is the scariest thing I've come across in business. You need to get rid of it, and fast.

## Customer

To be classified as a customer, your prospect needs to have spent money or done business with you, and you need to have recorded the sale in your records. This last step may seem strange, but it is most important because it allows you to differentiate between prospects and customers on your database. You see, if you are planning to send a letter out to all prospects offering them an incentive to buy, you don't want to be sending it to people who are already customers. This record will also tell you when they last bought, how often they buy, and what their average dollar sale is.

## Member

When your customers feel like they belong, they become members. They now have a feeling of belonging. Understand that customers who make two purchases are 10 times more likely to make more than those who have made only one. So, you need to put some effort into your members. Give them a membership card and a membership pack. How many of your customers know all your products? Very few, I would suggest. So why not include a product catalog in the membership pack? You can also include samples, vouchers, and things like that. One interesting example I came across recently was at a truck stop in New Zealand. The owner pinned up photographs on a notice board of all drivers who had stopped the night there. Then there's the coffee shop that gives you your own personalized coffee mug. Each time you come in, they get your mug down from the shelf for you. These are just two examples of how you can give members a sense of belonging. What else can you do? Can you think of anything that would be unique in your industry? Can you think of anything that would give you a marketing advantage?

## Advocate

Once you have members, you need to move them up the ladder to the next level—to that of advocate. An advocate is someone who sells you to other people. The criteria for being an advocate are that they will give referrals or promote you, and that they keep buying. Advocates are one of your major capital assets.

## Raving Fan

Once you have created advocates, you need to move them up to the top of the ladder where they become Raving Fans. Understand the difference: an advocate is someone who will sell for you, whereas a Raving Fan is someone who simply can't stop selling for you. The exciting thing about Raving Fans is that they can almost be regarded as part of your team. They want to see you succeed. Of course, they continue buying from you all along.

Remember, the aim of the game is to move people up from customer to Raving Fan. It's at this level where you really begin to make profit.

## Part 5

# ■ The Strategies

Once you've made the decision to build a referral-based business, there are a number of things you need to do that will get things moving for you. These I call strategies, and I will deal with them in detail shortly.

Bear in mind that the strategies that follow are *Action* strategies—they are meant to be implemented and used. Involve your team; let them know what you are doing and why. Consider them partners here because they will be active participants from here on.

Bear in mind, too, that the first six strategies *must* be implemented with each and every one that follows. Failure to do so will result in your not getting the number or quality of referrals you are looking for.

Work through the 21 Killer Referral Strategies that follow and make notes in the space provided. This will ensure that you remember things that might strike you as you read—it's highly likely that you will recognize particular facets of the strategies that apply to your business. Make notes, too, of other thoughts that occur to you, as these very often give rise to unique strategies or variations of them that could give you the edge over your opposition.

So what are the strategies?

Let's go right to them and see just what they can achieve for your business. Let's do this by viewing them by way of Charlie, my mechanic, who desperately wanted to change the way he went about his business at Charlie's Garage.

## *Action* Strategy Number 1

**You need to decide who your ideal customer is, and who you actually want referred to your business.**

Getting referrals that don't turn into business aren't referrals at all—they are just a nuisance. And so are referrals that only buy once from you. If you are getting the wrong types of referrals, chances are they will create more headaches for you than sales and never give you the business you are after.

For this reason you have to decide right now and up front, before you even begin to think about referral strategies, who it is you ideally want referred to you.

It's time for you to sit down and set the rules. You see, if you don't, your customers will do it for you.

If this should come as something of a surprise, don't worry; it's perfectly acceptable for you to decide whom you want to do business with. It is your business after all, isn't it? But if you're still a little skeptical, read on.

You'll always get the customers you're willing to accept.

If you've always accepted everyone who walked into your business with a dollar or two to spend, maybe you've already learned the lesson. But if you haven't, let me show it to you.

Some of the customers you deal with are more trouble than they're worth.

There will be those who actually cost you money every time you deal with them. I'm sure you now know what I'm talking about, because we've all experienced them.

Can you actually afford not to deal with anyone? Absolutely, because if most of your customers cost you money and you keep dealing with them, the simple truth is you'll end up going broke.

So what do you do about it?

Have you heard of the 80:20 rule? This is sometimes called the Pareto Principle. It states that 20 percent of your business comes from 80 percent of your customers. The flip side of this is that 80 percent of your headaches will generally come from 20 percent of your customers.

I got Charlie to sit down and begin thinking about the qualities he was looking for in a customer. This is what he came up with:

They pay their bills on time.

They are pleasant to deal with.

They are happy to pay my listed or quoted prices.

They refer their friends to me.

They are local customers.

They are regular customers.

They spend a lot with me.

They upgrade on a regular basis.

They make use of my after-sales service.

They buy auxiliary equipment from me.

They are happy to be on my mailing list.

They take advantage of my special events and sales.

They don't have their cars serviced by my competitors.

They are Raving Fans of Charlie's Garage.

There might be other qualities that are more specific to your business or industry. Can you think of any?

Now build up your list here:

**MY IDEAL CUSTOMER HAS THESE QUALITIES**

_____

_____

_____

_____

_____

_____

_____

Now it's time to jot down your thoughts, ideas, and comments before you forget them. Use the lines below for this.

**MY *ACTION* STEPS ARE:**

_____

_____

_____

_____

_____

_____

_____

# *Action* Strategy Number 2

> Time to go through your current customer list with your "ideal" customer criteria in mind.

The next thing you need to do is to grade your existing customers in one of four categories: A, B, C, or D.

An example of an A-grade customer is someone who pays his bills on time, is pleasant to deal with, is happy to pay your marked prices, sends his friends to do business with you, and spends a reasonable amount of money with you each year. You'd source these qualities from your ideal customer list you compiled for the previous strategy.

B-grade customers aren't quite the perfect or model customers, but they are still well worth having. They might be a little more price conscious, yet they still pay on time every time.

C-grade customers would probably be the type who would bring back goods for a refund just because they'd changed their mind, would haggle for as big a discount as they could get every time, would never listen to your advice, and would probably miss payment dates if you had an account facility.

D-grade customers are the ones you wished you never had. They are the ones that like creating a scene in your shop, especially when there are other customers nearby. They probably treat you and your team like dirt, always complaining about how expensive you are and how you never have what they want. You might even have suspected them of shoplifting at some stage, even though you might not have been able to prove it at the time.

The simple truth of the matter is this: when you decide whom you want to do business with, they'll start to show up.

My advice is this: Don't put up with customers who won't pay their bills, don't treat you well, and constantly hassle you on price. These customers will generally refer similar types of people to you, and that's the last thing you want to happen.

To get rid of your D-grade customers, simply send them a letter asking them to deal with someone else. Explain to them that you can't afford to deal with them any more.

Here's the letter Charlie wrote:

---

Dear Mr. and Mrs. Smith,

I am writing because I want to inform you of changes we are making to Charlie's Garage.

You see, we are determined to sharpen our focus on our valued customers so that we can continue to offer them the best service, the best prices, and the best products we possibly can.

After careful thought and consideration, and as a result of an in-house study to find out what most of our valued customers want, we will be implementing the following changes from the beginning of next month:

- The phasing out of our in-house account facility

- A change in the Garage's appearance, layout, and background music

- Centralized reception facility so that customers deal only with the customer liaison assistant and not the mechanics

- Discontinuance of the entry-level service and maintenance plan

- No more discounts—but the lowest prices for cash

- No more sales

As you can see, we will be repositioning the Garage up-market because this is the clear message we've received from our most valued customers.

Thank you for doing business with us in the past. I'm sure you will soon find another garage where you can have your car serviced, as there are many in this neighborhood.

Yours sincerely,

Charlie

---

Remember, it takes only one bad customer to ruin your entire day. And you can either ruin or make the day of your other customers by how you're feeling when you serve them. So take the time to decide on the qualities you want your new customers to have before you put strategies in place to attract them.

By the way, you may need to do a little self-analysis at this point. Ask yourself whether your new customers would want to do business with you. Or look at it from another viewpoint: what do you need to change to have them want to do business with you?

Your C-grade customers will meet just one or two or your criteria and need to be sent a fairly strong letter to inform them of the new rules of doing business with you. This is how Charlie handled it:

---

Dear Mr. and Mrs. Smith,

I am writing because I want you to be among the first to know about changes we are introducing to Charlie's Garage. That's right, things are moving here and we are excited.

You see, we are determined to sharpen our focus on our most valued customers so that we can continue to offer them the best service, the best prices, and the best products we possibly can.

After careful thought and consideration, and as a result of an in-house study to find out what most of our valued customers want, we will be implementing the following changes from the beginning of next month:

- The phasing out of our in-house account facility

- A change in the Garage's appearance, layout, and background music

- Centralized reception facility so that customers deal only with the customer liaison assistant and not the mechanics

- Discontinuance of the entry-level service and maintenance plan

- No more discounts—but the lowest prices for cash

- No more sales

---

As you can see, we will be repositioning the Garage up-market because this is the clear message received from our most valued customers.

If the above changes should inconvenience you, we will be more than happy to suggest an alternative garage, which may better suit your future needs and requirements.

Yours sincerely,

Charlie

Some will abide by the new rules while others will want to go elsewhere. Either way, once you've moved all your C and D customers out, your next step will be to train your B-grade customers how to become A-grade customers. This is easily done, again with a simple letter. Here's what Charlie wrote:

Dear Mr. and Mrs. Smith,

As you know, we have listened to what our most valued customers have been telling us, and we have taken action.

From now on you will see the difference; you will know what it's like to be an A-grade customer at Charlie's Garage. That's right, in return for your valued business, we will be treating you like the valued customer you really are. And you'll feel the difference. No more waiting to be served, no more waiting at the office to pay, and no more hassling by the mechanics. Our VIP advisors already know you by name and will be assisting you in the most unobtrusive manner possible when you next come in. Our up-to-date computerized billing system will know who you are when you enter the store, making checkout time effortless. You see, this system knows your preferences because it tracks your every visit, so you can be assured your requirements will always be taken into account.

As you can see, Mr. and Mrs. Smith, being an A-grade customer really counts. And I'm sure you'd like your family and friends to also become A-grade customers of ours too. But before you ask, the answer is *yes,* we'd love to have them. All you have to tell them is the following:

- We don't have an in-house account facility
- We have a centralized reception facility so that customers deal only with the customer liaison assistant and not the mechanics
- We do not have an entry-level service and maintenance plan
- We do not offer discounts—but the lowest prices for cash
- We do not hold sales

When your referrals arrive, tell them to ask for me personally; it will be my pleasure to show them around our modern workshop facility.

Yours sincerely,

Charlie

By the way, if you are reading this and thinking it doesn't apply to you because you don't have a list of past customers, be sure to read *Action* Strategy Number 5.

Let your A-grade customers know you can now devote far more time to taking care of their needs, more time and energy to give them better service, and of course, to ask them for several referrals.

Remember that if you give great service to D-grade customers, they'll generally refer more D-grade customers to you. You want referrals from your A-grade customers, not the D-grade ones. The people you love to do business with, the people who meet your criteria for being a customer, the people with A-grade referrals, are the ones you should be chasing.

By the time you've completed this exercise, every client will be aware of the type of customers you want to deal with. The most important message you need to get through to them is that you're doing this in order to provide the best service possible for your target market.

One final point here: you might be wondering who will cater for D-grade customers if every business were to only chase A-grade customers. Well, every business is different. They all have different expectations of their clients. What you might regard as an A-grade customer another business might class as C-grade. It all depends on your business, your own criteria, and your own business experiences with your customers.

Now it's time once more to write down your thoughts and ideas on what you have just read.

## MY *ACTION* STEPS ARE:

_____

_____

_____

_____

_____

_____

_____

## *Action* Strategy Number 3

**Work out how much each and every one of your customers has cost you.**

I want to focus on a new way of thinking about your customers and your marketing. From here on in I want you to see things from another perspective—one that will make all the difference in the way you operate from this point on.

Every time you get a new customer, I want you to be aware of how much that customer costs you. I want you to be aware that you have in actual fact just bought that customer.

That's right; I want you to understand that you have really just "bought" that new customer. Think of this as your marketing cost. This way you will understand the need to make your investment back as the customer spends money with you.

This may be a refreshing approach, but it's also a very realistic one. You see, each and every customer does cost you money initially through all the advertising and promotion you have to do to reach him. In other words, you buy your customers by virtue of the fact that they cost you money just to get them through the door. The essence of your marketing campaign is to keep reducing the amount you have to pay for new customers, because the unit cost comes down as the number of new customers each campaign brings in increases.

For example, let's assume you advertise in the local paper and your ad costs you $500 each week. Let's suppose that, on average, this ad brings in 10 new customers a week. Each new customer would therefore be costing you $50.

Once you know this information, you have various options to choose from. The first you'd probably consider is to put in place strategies to reduce the price you pay for each new customer. What you would essentially be doing in this case is looking at ways to reduce your marketing cost per customer. How would you go about this? You'd probably look at doing one of two things—or both if you were really smart. You could try writing a more targeted or specific ad, or you could try selling more to each prospect that calls in response to the ad.

Let me give you a great piece of advice: don't just make your business profitable; make every single customer profitable. This is one of the great secrets of running a successful business. Can you now see why it's important to deal only with A-grade customers?

So let's now work out how much each customer you've got actually costs you in the first place. But be warned; the results will surprise you. It may even come as something of a shock. This is what you do to work this out:

Go back through your records and add up the number of new customers you've dealt with over the past month, six months, or year. If you don't have the records or if you can't narrow it down to just new customers, take an educated guess at how many of your customers represent repeat business.

Add up all your sales, promotion, marketing, and other associated costs you have incurred over that period to bring in new customers to your business.

Add up your daily overheads. I suggest writing off this figure to your new customers because sales to past or existing customers (but not new customers) will be seen as pure profit, allowing you to know when your new customers become profitable to you. My experience has shown that new customers aren't profitable until they have come back and bought somewhere between two and three times. Isn't that useful to know?

Add steps two and three together. This is your total customer acquisition cost.

Divide the total acquisition cost by the number of new customers you have. The answer will be how much each new customer costs you.

Got that? Right. Now it's time for you to work out how much each new customer costs you. Just fill in the blanks in the following form.

## COST PER CUSTOMER

1. **No. of New Customers per Month:**  _____

2. Monthly Sales Cost:  _____

3. Monthly Promotions Cost:  _____

4. Monthly Marketing Cost:  _____

5. Monthly Additional Marketing Costs:  _____

6. **Total Marketing Cost:** (2+3+4+5)  _____

7. Monthly Rent:  _____

8. Monthly Communications Costs:  _____

9. Monthly Electricity Cost:  _____

10. Monthly Salaries, Commissions, etc.:  _____

11. Monthly Transport Costs:  _____

12. Monthly Production Costs:  _____

13. Monthly Sundry Costs:  _____

14. **Total Monthly Overheads:** (7+8+9+10+11+12+13)  _____

**Cost Per Customer = (6 + 14) ÷ 1**

Of course, if you want to work out your annual figure, you'd use annual and not monthly figures in the calculation.

I got Charlie to run through this exercise, and this is what he came up with:

---

### COST PER CUSTOMER

| | | |
|---|---|---:|
| 1. | **No. of New Customers per Month:** | 25 |
| 2. | Monthly Promotions Cost: | $2,250 |
| 3. | Monthly Marketing Cost: | $3,000 |
| 4. | **Total Marketing Cost:** (2+3) | **$5,250** |
| 5. | Monthly Rent: | $10,000 |
| 6. | Monthly Communications Costs: | $750 |
| 7. | Monthly Electricity Cost: | $550 |
| 8. | Monthly Salaries, Commissions, etc: | $15,000 |
| 9. | Monthly Transport Costs: | $2,000 |
| 10. | Monthly Sundry Costs: | $1,000 |
| 11. | **Total Monthly Overheads:** (5+6+7+8+9+10) | **$29,300** |

**Cost Per Customer = (4 + 11) ÷ 1    $5,250 + $29,300 / 25 = $1,382**

---

If you're surprised at how much you've been paying for each new customer, or the fact that you make a loss on the first sale to a new customer, then that's great. At least now you'll realize why you can't just race in and get referrals; you first have to do the numbers.

Can you now see why you need to bring each new customer back two or three times before you begin to make a profit from her?

If these numbers have shocked you, take heart. At least now you have the numbers upon which to base the decisions you make in the future. You'll at least be able to base your business on something concrete rather than just a stab in the dark.

So take the time to work out these numbers as accurately as you can—they'll make a huge difference to the way you do business in the future.

Make notes now about this strategy and how it may apply to your business.

## MY *ACTION* STEPS ARE:

_____

_____

_____

_____

_____

_____

_____

## *Action* Strategy Number 4

**Decide how much you are willing to invest to "buy" your new customers.**

Now that you know how much you've spent buying new customers in the past, you need to work out how much you can afford to spend with your referral campaigns in the future. You see, if you build a referral-based business, this is how you'll be buying your customers.

This step is important because I have discovered through coaching literally thousands of businesses all over the world that very few of them launch marketing campaigns without having any real idea of just how much they can afford to spend to buy new customers. And it really doesn't matter what type of business you run or how elaborate your marketing campaign is; the fact remains that you need to know before you start how much you can afford.

Even microbusinesses engage in some form of marketing, even if they are unaware that they are doing so. The more you know about your costs, the better you can plan and manage your business. It's as simple as that.

So, where do you start? Working out how much you can spend on your new customers actually starts by looking at how much your average customers will spend with you over the course of their lifetimes.

Let's make use of an example here and go back to Charlie's Garage. This is how he did it:

I started by asking him this: "How much is your average customer worth over a lifetime of buying from you, Charlie?"

Have *you* ever thought to think about your customers this way? I wouldn't be surprised if the answer is *no* because that's the answer I usually get when I ask my coaching clients this. And this was the answer I got from Charlie.

"How on earth would I find this out, Brad?" he asked. This was my reply:

"The simplest way you can find this out, Charlie, is by sampling your customer base. Look at a group of your past customers, taking into account the best and worst of them, then average out how much each has spent with you and how much profit you have made from each."

If you don't have any specific records of past sales, don't worry; there are ways to arrive at a suitable answer.

This is what you do:

- Work out how long your average customer stays with you. Of course, some will only ever buy once, while others will stay with you forever. What you are interested in here is the average.

- Find the average number of sales you make to each customer. Again, don't be too put off if you don't have accurate information from which to work. It's only an average you are looking for.

- Multiply 1 with 2 above and consider the answer. Is it realistic? If not, then you need to readdress your averages in steps 1 and 2. If the answer proves to be a very small amount or if it is just one or two purchases, then make sure you read *Action* Strategy Number 5 very carefully.

- Work out how much profit you make, on average, on your *first sale* to a new customer. Remember this: you need to know this or every referral could end up costing you profits.

This is what Charlie discovered when he ran through this exercise:

- His average customer stays with him for 7 years.

- The average number of sales he makes to each customer is 7.

- Each customer deals with him 49 times over the course of his lifetime.

- His average profit from the first sale, after taking into account his customer acquisition cost, came as a huge shock. These were his figures:

  Average Dollar sale:     $680
  Average profit:          $220
  Profit on 1st sale  = acquisition cost − average profit
                      = $1382 − $220
                      = −$1162

Now that you know how much your customers are worth to you over a lifetime of buying, how much profit you make on a first sale, and how much your past customers have cost you, it's time to make an informed decision about how much you can invest to buy new customers.

I find the easiest way to do this is through a series of pointed questions. Think carefully and answer honestly. And remember, your need to think of your customers as an investment you have to sink money into before you can get a return.

So, what type of questions do you need to ask, and answer?

Here's my list:

1. Do I have to make a profit on the first sale?

2. Can I make up the profit in future sales if I don't make a profit in the first one?

3. If I give something away as a referral tool, what conversion rate do I need in order to make a profit?

This list isn't all-inclusive; there could be other factors that better suit your own particular industry or situation. Remember, the more questions you ask yourself, the better your final decision is likely to be.

Remember, too, that what we are talking about here is the hard-dollar cost that you can invest, not the perceived value of the customer of what it is you are selling. There is a difference here—an important difference.

Time to make a few notes once more.

## MY *ACTION* STEPS ARE:

_____

_____

_____

_____

_____

_____

_____

## *Action* Strategy Number 5

> Be sure to keep in touch with your customers at least every three months.

If you read diligently through this book, make notes, and implement strategies that will transform your business into a referral-based business, you'll be serious about getting referrals, won't you? And seeing you'll be going to a lot of trouble and effort to achieve this, I want to be sure that you understand that real marketing is more than just reducing the costs of bringing new customers into your business.

It's also very much about using your marketing skills to increase the average lifetime value of your past customers.

The best way to achieve this is by keeping in touch with them.

Time to let you in on a little secret. This may astound you, but what is even more surprising to me is that it's such a huge waste of money—such a huge, needless waste. The average businesses I come across spend five times more money on trying to get *new* customers coming into their businesses for the first time than they do on keeping the *old* ones coming back.

Understand that this absolute waste of valuable resources will become glaringly evident when you think about your customers from a lifetime value point of view. If you're not proactive in your approach to business—if you don't ask your customers to come back and do business with you again—then why should they?

Think about it for a moment. Does this sound more than just familiar? Is this how you've been running your business until now? If so, you're not alone because this is how the vast majority of businesses operate.

But if you're starting to feel uncomfortable about how much potential business you've been blowing out the window each and every month, then it's time to get positive and do something about it.

Start by thinking about how easy it really is to increase your level of business by just doing the opposite of what you have been doing up until now.

Consider this scenario. It concerns Charlie and should give you a great idea about how easy it is to get your existing customers to come back and spend more with you rather than with your competitor.

Charlie wrote a simple newsletter and mailed it out to all his customers every two or three months. In it he advertised special offers that were available only through his newsletter. He also mailed out Easter, birthday, and Christmas cards to all his clients just to stay in touch, to let them know he was thinking of them. How much do you think a small gesture like that will increase their lifetime value?

You see, if you remember them, chances are they will remember you, and if you are building a referral-based business, this is all-important. People simply can't refer people to someone they don't remember! The rule here is that if you want to keep building the relationship, then you need to communicate regularly with your past customers.

OK, so Charlie was communicating with his past customers, what does he have to do next to maximize his chances of getting referrals from them?

He gives them exceptional service.

This is a non-negotiable element that you simply have to do if you want to create a supersuccessful business. But here's another astonishing fact that may surprise you. Every study I've read shows that when people purchase from you three times or more, they'll be at least 10 times more likely to refer their friends to you. Now isn't that interesting?

This referral strategy sounds simple enough and it is, but many I suggest it to ask whether it is overly expensive. Here's another surprise. My experience is that it costs in the region of $12 a year to build a great relationship with each customer by writing to them once a month. And if you wanted to write to them only every three months, it would only cost you $4 per customer.

If you have a great record-keeping system and had people's e-mail addresses, then the cost would be very much less than that. Group e-mails are one of the great innovations of recent times, but do get people's permission before including them on any e-mail database. All you need to do is explain to them that you'd like to include them in the distribution list for your regular e-mail newsletter. This way they'll get to hear first about any new products being offered, any great promotions or sales, and any special deals you'll be offering for your A-grade customers.

Here's another thing I've learned by running my own referral-based business: the numbers do add up. In fact, I've found that you can't possibly do business and expect to make a great profit without keeping in touch with each and every one of your customers.

If you don't bother to build the relationship, you're throwing away "real" profits. Take the time to build a database and take the time to use it. Communicate with your customers as often as you think feasible. Only then will getting new customers through referrals really pay off.

Are there any ideas that came to you as you read through this strategy? Have you had any inspirational ideas? If so, be sure to write them down now before you forget them.

## MY *ACTION* STEPS ARE:

_____

_____

_____

_____

_____

_____

_____

_____

## *Action* Strategy Number 6

**Teach your customers why it's good for them to give you referrals.**

Every time you market your business and communicate with customers it comes down to what I call the proverbial radio station WII-FM.

Confused?

WII-FM stands for "What's In It For Me." This is just human nature. Your customers will want to know why they should do things for you, they'll want to know how they'll be affected when they take action, and, most of all, they'll want to know what they'll get in return.

Why should they, after all, be expected to do something for you for nothing? You don't give them extra special prices just because they are your customers. You don't regularly give them something for nothing just for the fun of it or because you like them, so why should they?

When you're running your business in a proactive fashion and actively chasing referrals, you need to take this into account. It may only be that the customers' knowledge that they've helped friends find something they need is all the customers receive in return. But if this is the case, you still need to make this clear to them at the outset.

You need to teach your existing customers (as well as any new ones you pick up from now on) why it's good for them to give referrals. What you'll be aiming at is educating them about how referring people to you can, and will, help them in return. I know this may sound like a cliché, but it really is important. We'll get into detail about the rewards you can give them in return for referrals later on in this book, but for now, take a look at what Charlie does. He just tells them the simple logic I've used so successfully many times before in my own businesses.

This is what Charlie tells them:

1. By referring new clients, they're helping Charlie's Garage save marketing dollars, which allows him to pass on to his customers greater savings, greater rewards, and better service.

2. They're making sure Charlie has a strong and healthy business, which increases the chances of his being around in the future when they might again need him to service or repair their cars.

3. They're helping Charlie work with only the best level of customers so he can always come up with new ways of serving them better.

Every time you educate a customer about referring new people to you, you get an advocate for life in return, with one condition: you need to make sure you always give them the level of service you promised. It doesn't have to be five-star, just what you originally promised.

And don't forget to tell your customers that you are after quality referrals just like them. You see, by doing so you'll not only be giving them a compliment, you'll also be setting the standard regarding who they should refer to you.

These first six strategies are a must with any of the other referral strategies I'll be discussing from here on. Regard them as non-negotiable. Make them part of your daily routine. Build them into your system. Doing so will give you a solid base upon which to build your new referral-based business before you begin asking for new referrals.

Educating your customers about referring people to you is simple, and ultimately very profitable. But remember to give them more than one reason and more than one benefit for referring their friends to you.

Can you add to this? Can you think of any more great reasons why your customers' friends should do business with you? Can you think of any more compelling reasons why your customers should refer others to you?

If you can, jot them down now.

## MY *ACTION* STEPS ARE:

_____

_____

_____

_____

_____

_____

_____

## *Action* Strategy Number 7

> **Give awesome service that creates "delighted advocates" instead of satisfied customers.**

There are really only two reasons you'll tell your friends about a business you've dealt with: because you've had really bad service there or because their service was outstanding.

If you think about it, it's most unlikely that you'd ever bother telling your friends about a business if the service you received was just average. The same would be true if it was just satisfactory. You see, the vast majority of businesses do OK when it comes to service; they do what they and you expect them to do, but how many of them do you talk about afterwards? The answer is, of course, very few, simply because if you had to talk about every shop you went into, every business you dealt with, you'd probably have little time left in which to do the other things you need to in your day.

It's surprising just how many people and businesses we deal with on a daily basis. This not only means most businesses have a huge job on their hands if they want to leave a lasting impression of the minds of their customers, it also means that there is a great opportunity for those who are serious about marketing themselves in a simple yet meaningful way.

By the way, if a business gives satisfactory service, would you say it was performing well? What does the word "satisfactory" actually mean in business terms? I'd like to suggest it means that they are giving their customers all that they want, but *nothing more.*

Now I know there are many businesses that don't seem to ever use the words *customer* and *service* in the same sentence, but I'm not talking about them here. That topic has been covered more extensively in my book *Instant Sales.* If you want to build a referral-based business, then I'm taking for granted that you give great customer service at the very least. What I'm aiming at achieving through this book is to get you to raise the customer service bar in your business to the next level: to being absolutely awesome.

You see, to really delight people, to have them really *rave* about you, you need to give them much more than they expect. You need to give them more than they ever thought you could give them. You need to give them *awesome service.*

To put it simply, you need to be amazing. You need to do something that people will want to tell their friends about.

Let's think about this for a minute.

Think back to great experiences you have had in the past. You know the businesses that have given you outstanding service before. What did they do that made you believe they had given you exemplary service? Can you put your finger on it or was it something less tangible?

Now think what you can learn from that experience. Is there anything you can emulate in your own business? Are there any concepts you can adapt? How can you follow in their footsteps by providing that same level of service to your customers? How can you go one step further and improve on it? What do you have to do to provide awesome service?

Now it's time to get into *Action* again. It's time for you to jot down a list of things you can do to achieve this. Here's an example of what Charlie does:

## CHARLIE'S AWESOME SERVICE STRATEGY

- When giving quotes, send a courier package about my business timed to arrive before I do to quote for the job.

- When sending parcels through the post, include a small bag of sweets with it.

- Send each customer a small gift through the mail the day after they've had their car serviced.

- When calling on fleet owners to solicit their business, take morning tea to their offices.

- When providing after-sales service, do it in such a way that that people will always comment on it.

The best thing about giving awesome service is that it really doesn't cost you anything for a simple smile, a warm greeting, a friendly good-bye, and any other gesture that shows you care. All it takes is a short letter, a small gift, or a quick phone call to do more than people expect.

One other thing: the more people you touch through awesome service, the bigger your referral sales team will be. That's right; you'll in effect have all these people working for you as salespeople.

Isn't that amazing?

So, now that you understand the truly awesome power that you can unleash just by ensuring you provide absolutely everyone with awesome service, what do you think your most profitable investment in business is?

Think about this for a while. What can you invest in that will yield the best profit? Technology? How about systems?

The best investment you can make by far is in people. That's right. You see, if you keep investing in great customer service, your customers will keep investing in you.

So my final message relating to this strategy is this: create lifelong relationships with your customers rather than just being satisfied with single sales and then bidding them good-bye.

## MY *ACTION* STEPS ARE:

_____

_____

_____

_____

_____

_____

_____

## *Action* Strategy Number 8

**Make sure you thank your customers and ask them to tell their friends about you.**

The easiest and best way to really make your customers feel special—to ask them to come back and to ask them to refer their friends to you—is simply to say "thanks."

Here's why it works so well. Just think back to how many times in the last six months you've received a thank-you note after you've made a purchase.

It's my guess the answer is probably none.

This is your opportunity. Because so few businesses do this, when *you* make the effort, people will consider it most unusual. They will take note and show it to their friends. And it will make an impression on their friends too, because chances are, it will be the first time they too have come across a gesture like this. They'll pass on your name and tell everyone the great story about how wonderful you are. This is word-of-mouth advertising at its most powerful.

The simple truth is that a simple thank-you note sent in the mail will get people talking about you for one good reason: nobody else does it.

So what do you do to make an impression when thanking a customer? How can you go about it?

Here are some ideas to start you thinking:

- Send each customer a small gift with your logo or emblem on it. And be sure it's not corporate junk. When choosing your gifts, ask yourself whether it's the type of gift you'd like to receive.

- Send your customers a box of chocolates or a bottle of wine. But remember to make sure you don't do this around Christmas time so as not to send them a confusing message.

- If they have bought a car from you, how about sending them a free car wash voucher or a set of headlight protectors?

- If it's clothing you sold them, a matching scarf, handkerchief, or pair of socks will be very well received.

- And if you sold them an alarm system, send them a personal alarm.

Get the idea? Now what can you do to make an impression? What unique features does your business have that would compliment a particular gift? Perhaps you market an item that would be perfect. Charlie sends each customer a can of oil the week after he's serviced their car.

But whatever you do, keep this in mind: if you give a gift to your customers as they make a purchase, it won't have the same impact as it would if you were to send it directly to their homes a few days later. You need to understand that when shoppers take their purchases home, they are usually excited by what they have bought. However, this excitement will have worn off within a few days. Their excitement will be sparked all over again when your thank-you note or simple gift arrives a few days later. When this happens you'll have the perfect opportunity to ask them to tell a few friends about you.

Here's an example of what Charlie says on his thank-you card:

---

Dear Mrs. Smith,

By the way, we thrive on working with people who are great to deal with, and yes, you're one of them.

For this reason I know you must have a few friends who are just like you, so please send them to us as soon as you can. We'll take great care of them for you.

Oh, and once again, thanks.

Charlie
Charlie's Garage

---

Using thank-you notes is a great way to ask for referrals, and it makes sure your customers are happy with their purchases, but perhaps more importantly, it's very effective.

Remember, if you don't take good care of your customers, then someone else most definitely will.

So, do you have any thoughts you'd like to make a note of? Do it now.

**MY *ACTION* STEPS ARE:**

_____

_____

_____

_____

_____

_____

_____

_____

## *Action* Strategy Number 9

**Just be daring. Ask for a referral when people buy from you (or even when they don't buy from you).**

Ask the right question and you'll always get the right answer. Sometimes it takes a few questions, but you'll get there when you test the questions you use.

I'm still amazed by the number of people who simply don't ask for referrals when their customers' emotions are running high and they're happiest to give them.

I'm even more amazed by the manner in which those who do get around to asking for referrals do it. You see, they do it in such a clumsy and awkward fashion that it's no surprise they don't get the result they are hoping for.

Asking for a referral is like asking for anything else. You need to choose your moment well and you need to talk with conviction. Don't feel shy. You're not begging for something you have no right to have.

Think of this as just another component of your sales pitch. Remember that all you are doing is communicating, meaning you are aiming to achieve two-way understanding with your customers. There's nothing unusual about that at all.

And because you are engaged in this two-way exchange of ideas and information, if you give good service to your customers, they will feel obliged to give you something even if they don't end up buying from you on this occasion. So ask for a referral. And if they do buy from you, remember that their emotions will be running high and they'll be most likely to refer someone to you if you ask the right questions.

What are the "right questions?" What do you need to bear in mind when asking them?

Here are my rules:

- Just asking for a referral without giving a reason why you want referrals is a waste of time.

- Ask for referrals after you've received a commitment for the sale but before you've finalized the details of the sale.

- Ask your customers why they decided to buy from you, and then ask them if they have any friends who would be inclined to buy for the same reason.

- Give your customers at least two valid reasons why they should give those people's names to you. Read Strategies 12 through 15 carefully for ideas.

Now here's something else where so many salespeople go wrong when asking for a referral: they think that when they receive a *no* response, it means *no*. Understand that it only means no *for now,* so don't close the door to the possibility of asking the question again later.

Another thing salespeople should bear in mind is this: when customers don't buy, they usually feel a little awkward about having to dream up an excuse for not buying. They very often don't want to say that they can't afford it just yet, or that they still need to shop around to see if they can find the same item cheaper elsewhere. If that salesperson were to sense the delicate position the customer is in, he could come to the customer's rescue and divert attention away from this issue by asking for a referral. This usually defuses the customers' pent-up emotions and gives them a way of changing the subject. It also helps restore their "pride" or "ego" by allowing them to regain the "upper emotional ground" by being able to hand over something other than money or an order. They feel their situation has been restored because they were ultimately able to hand over something that may prove to be far more valuable to the business than money— a good referral.

But it still requires tact on the part of the salesperson. The last thing the customers need is to have salt rubbed into their wounds. This is how the Charlie broaches the subject:

"Well, if you feel you don't want to have your engine overhauled at the moment, I understand. But you would probably know of a couple of people who are thinking of having their cars serviced at the moment. Would it be OK if I were to contact them now?"

People usually feel obliged to help you out in a situation like this because they have just said *no* to making a purchase from you.

My advice in situations like this is to take your time planning well how you are going to ask for a referral. Then be consistent—run through the same procedure with every customer you deal with.

But before you jump straight in and ask the first customer who says no to a sale, run this simple test through in your mind: *If you were a customer, would you pass your friends' details to you right now?* The answer you give may mean that you have to change a few things first to make certain that they'd want to refer family and friends to you. Write them down now.

## MY *ACTION* STEPS ARE:

_____

_____

_____

_____

_____

_____

_____

## *Action* Strategy Number 10

> **Let your customers know you'll be asking for referrals later on.**

Don't hit them cold—give them a chance to think about whom they want to refer.

I have found that setting your customers up for the opportunity to refer new customers to you in the future always proves worthwhile when you follow a few simple steps.

Imagine the scene: It's a quiet morning and customers haven't exactly been streaming in through the doors of Charlie's Garage. His three customer service people have been busying themselves by restocking and tidying the shelves in the reception area. Charlie has been catching up with paperwork that is fast becoming due.

Then all of a sudden the reception area is teaming with customers. Must be getting close to lunchtime, he reminds himself. His customer service people are quick off the mark, eager to notch up a few sales and to increase their personal tallies for the month.

Charlie looks up on hearing the doorbell ring once more, heralding the arrival of yet another customer. She looks around the reception area in the undecided manner of a new prospect. It is clearly her first time there.

Noticing that all his team members are engaged, he springs to his feet and makes his way over to where she is browsing.

It's now time for him to make the first move.

"Good morning. My name is Charlie and I am the owner of this garage," he says. "Before we get into what it is you require, I'd like to let you know how we work with our customers. Would that be OK?"

He pauses and waits for the answer, which will nearly always be in the affirmative.

"We get about 80 percent of our business from referrals and I like working with people just like you. So, what I'd like to ask is that if you believe you get value from working with me, you'll refer at least two people to me who are just like you. I'm not asking you for them now, but at some stage when you believe you've received great value. Would that be OK?"

Of course, you may decide not to use these exact words, but make sure you use the major points as outlined above in your script. You may decide to model your script along similar lines to this example, or you may decide to come up with something more original or uniquely yours. But whatever you decide, you must be comfortable with what you say and how you say it.

What you will be doing by letting your customers know up front that you will be asking them for referrals is getting the rules of your relationship clear before you begin doing business. This way people will feel more comfortable and will want to refer others to you.

You see, if you give your customer something to think about after the sale has taken place, you'll have set them up to begin thinking of whom they should refer. They'll also begin thinking about the purchase they are going to make.

Here's another useful tip: Sometimes when you give somebody something and then take it away from them, they want it even more. Do you know what I mean? The same can be true here. Once you've mentioned that you will be seeking referrals later on, you then can change your mind and say you're not so sure if you will be taking on any more referrals at this stage.

Now let's go back to Charlie's Garage and hear how he would handle this.

"I've been giving it second thoughts," he'd say. "I'm beginning to think I may have been overly hasty in asking for a referral from you. You see, we have been inundated with referrals lately, and quite honestly, I only want to take on referrals if we can guarantee the same fantastic level of service that our current customers enjoy. I'd really hate to disappoint new customers by not being able to live up to their expectations."

Nine times out of 10 they will beg you to squeeze in just one more referral.

This isn't the only strategy you could use to get referrals from your customers. There are as many as you can think up. You could give customers a referral form to fill out when they are back at home. Remember, your overriding aim here is to get referrals by giving *awesome* service—something that will get people talking. In this case, you wouldn't rely on customers to return the forms next time they shop or are in the area because you'd then be leaving too much to chance. You'd let your customers know that you will be calling at their homes to personally collect the form. This will surprise them and get them talking. It will also be unique. Chances are they will not have come across this level of service before. And in many cases, they'll ask you not to go to so much trouble; they'll save you the journey by filling in the form then and there.

One thing to remember when you're asking for referrals—*it's all about your attitude.*

If you have it in your mind that you are "milking" them, then that will be what they perceive. Be genuine and honest; if you are, you'll get the referrals you want.

One last tip about letting people know you'll be asking for referrals: Consider stating this in your marketing material. For example, the introductory marketing material you send out should mention that customers who receive great value usually refer several of their friends to the business.

Now, before you press on to the next strategy, it's time to write down some notes about what you can say to customers to get them prepared to make referrals.

## MY *ACTION* STEPS ARE:

_____

_____

_____

_____

_____

_____

_____

## *Action* Strategy Number 11

**Make giving you a few referrals a condition of doing business with you.**

When you set up your business, you make the rules for people doing business with you. Not setting any rules means they will set them for you.

If you really want to have a business that just runs on referrals, then make it a rule that for people to do business with you, they have to give you referrals.

There are several ways of introducing this to your customers, but one thing you must do is to make it very clear to them up front. Here are some methods Charlie has used successfully in the past, and some that I have used also. Introduce the concept by giving each customer a copy of your Commitment Statement. This is a document that sets out what you, as a business, will do for your customers in return for their making certain commitments to you. Here's a copy of *Action International's* Commitment Statement:

### *ACTION INTERNATIONAL* CLIENT COMMITMENT STATEMENT

As a client of *Action International* it is important that we have your commitment and dedication to the implementation of the marketing systems designed for you over the next 12 months. To ensure that we can deliver the systems to you, we ask you to please make note of the following standards and commit with your signature at the bottom indicating your commitment to the program.

You are prepared to invest in yourself and meet your commitment with *Action International* every month, on time, so that we can continue to provide the service to build your business.

You will offer honest feedback at all times. This includes giving praise when we've helped you achieve the results your after, and offering suggestions, *not attacking*, should we make a mistake.

You will be honest, truthful, and up front with us at all times.

You accept that the program you have committed to is a 12-month program, and that success does not happen overnight.

You are committed to keeping all your appointments with *Action International* and will be prepared to give at least 24 hours' notice if you are unable to keep an appointment. If you do not notify us of any changes to your appointments, you accept that you will forgo that consultation.

If we call and leave a message for you or send a fax, you will acknowledge this communication with us before the end of the next working day. We will also display this courtesy.

You will disclose *all* necessary information to the *Action International* team so that we can service you efficiently.

You will be realistic with your expectations of us and of yourself.

You will be prepared to work to achieve your goals and you will cooperate with *Action International* at all times.

You are prepared to change to achieve your goals.

You will take action on any strategy or suggestion that we make (given that it is reasonable to do so at the time) and ensure that you undertake to test these concepts or idea's to see the various test results and determine what works best for your business.

Signed _____

Date _____

- Charlie produced an audiotape that outlines how he works with new customers and why they should give him referrals.

- Charlie tells his customers about this rule face-to-face before he services their car for the first time. But he makes sure to give them an easy way to get the referrals to him. Think this through before putting this strategy into place.

- Charlie accepts only customers who are referred to him by current customers. Of course, his past or existing customers should have already let them know what the rules are for doing business with him.

- Charlie also takes the bold approach of advertising the fact that he deals only with people who have been referred to him. This gives him an air of exclusivity, which in itself makes certain people want to deal with him. His marketing pieces outline why he operates this way and what the benefits are to his customers.

- Some referral-based businesses send out only products ordered by customers *after* they have handed in their referrals.

So, how keen are you to make your business buzz by changing the way you get customers? Do these possibilities excite you? If you decide to adopt this approach—making referrals a condition of doing business with you—then there are a few conditions that apply. They are the following:

- Your business has to be giving *awesome* customer service from the very moment each and every customer first contacts you.

- Your business will be selling *value* rather than discount.

- Your customers aren't *competing* with each other.

Think long and hard about the above points. Do you meet the criteria? If not, can you change things so that you do? Jot down your thoughts in the space provided below.

If you're still not certain, bear in mind that if you get just one new customer from every customer you deal with, your business will regularly keep doubling in size.

Can you claim to be growing at this rate at present? Does your business grow this strongly the way it's being run right now? Can you see the potential of building a referral-based business?"

If you have been working your way diligently through this book until now, it means you have been setting yourself up to handle a whole lot more business in the future. Isn't that thought exciting?

Now it's time once more for you to make any additional notes that may come in handy later on.

## MY *ACTION* STEPS ARE:

_____

_____

_____

_____

_____

_____

_____

## *Action* Strategy Number 12

Reward your customers with a special price if they give you a certain number of "qualified" referrals.

If you are going to buy new customers for your business, why not buy them from your past customers? In other words, you can give your past and present customers the rewards as a direct discount on their purchase.

Think of it this way: You're probably going to be spending money sourcing new customers through advertising and promotion anyway, but in a referral-based business where you don't have these costs (or at least you have very small marketing-related costs), you could still budget to "spend" this money by offsetting it against the price your customers would normally pay.

You can give them the discount up front, send them a gift check for each referral, or credit their accounts when they next purchase from you. Either way you'll be giving your customers a "one-time" chance to receive a great deal and help you out at the same time.

Just think of the marketing advantage this approach will give you. Where else would your customers be able to actually "earn" money just for referring a few friends? They'll see it as doing them a favor, because those friends will then also be able to earn some money (or get some extra-special deals) when their turn comes to make a few referrals.

What Charlie says is this: "Would you like to pay the regular price for your car's service, or would you prefer the discounted referral price?" How powerful is that?

The usual reply he receives goes something like this: "Can you please explain what you mean by the referral price?"

This opens the way for him to outline his strategy and why it's in their interest to make a few referrals. He explains the reasons why he gives a discount when someone gives him a referral. He shows them what he would otherwise be spending on marketing and how he can rather pass on these savings to them if he doesn't need to spend big on marketing.

The best example of this that I have come across was a security company that offered a $100 discount off the price of a new alarm system if the customer gave it the names of 20 people who would fit their target market.

Just think what your customers are going to say to everyone when they get back home! Adapt this strategy and you will get a large number of referrals very quickly.

Of course, buying referrals is a much better option than buying new prospects through the usual marketing methods because it allows you to tell each new prospect that one of their friends asked you to call her.

But before you rush out and implement a similar strategy, make sure you first test and measure to find out your average conversion rate (the number of people you are able to convert from being just a prospect to becoming a customer by buying from you) before you go ahead and offer large bonuses. If you understand what your conversion rate is, you will at least be certain that you are investing wisely to attract new customers.

I realize this may sound like an expensive strategy, but you need to bear in mind that a discount on a purchase of any amount is really only your hard cost of that amount. What I mean by this is best explained with an example.

Let's assume you are offering a $100 discount on a security system. To be able to knock $100 off the price might only cost you $40 or $50 in hard costs to buy those 20 new leads. This puts a whole new perspective on it, doesn't it?

The thing to do when deciding what you should do and how much you can realistically afford is to first work out how much you want to spend on every new customer, and then to calculate what your conversion rate is. The answer will tell you the size of the discount you can afford to give.

Can you see the benefits, both to yourself as well as to your customers, of running a referral-based business? It's really a fantastic system because it relies on your customers being directly involved in your marketing activities, which makes sure you measure up to their expectations, and it rewards them directly without negatively affecting your cash flow situation at all.

The main point about Strategy Number 12 is to make sure you reward your customers and give them a real incentive for giving you referrals.

Is there anything you'd like to add?

## MY *ACTION* STEPS ARE:

_____

_____

_____

_____

_____

_____

_____

_____

## *Action* Strategy Number 13

> Offer your customers a gift, gift check, or even a free service for each referral.

The best way to get your customers to refer people to you is to offer them something for their troubles. One thing to bear in mind, though, is that what you are offering them doesn't jeopardize any sales you might make to them in the future.

Be aware that the gifts you give say as much about you as your marketing does. For this reason, every gift you give must add value to the relationship you have with your customers, and lead them to doing more business with you in the future.

When you give your customers a gift check that they can spend when making another purchase, you'll know you've bought future sales the moment you give it. You'll also know they will be coming back sometime to redeem it. When they do, all you have to do is up-sell them to make the visit even more profitable for you.

When you give customers a gift, make sure it compliments what you sell rather than being something that you sell. That way you won't be limiting your sales opportunities. What's the point of doing all the smart things to dramatically increase your client base, only to have them buy nothing from you because you are giving them what they need for free? Rather, offer them something they will value and come in to claim. This way they will be exposing themselves to other, more profitable, bread-and-butter lines you stock. When they see how your items complement what they have just been given, they will want to buy because this will make their gifts so much more usable, functional, or versatile. For example, if you ran a CD shop and gave away a good pair of surround sound speakers to every customer who referred 10 friends, customers might decide to buy a few CDs and a quality CD cleaning kit from you while they were in the shop collecting their speakers.

If you are a hairdresser, a lawn mowing person, or someone who provides some other regular service for customers, you can easily offer them a free haircut, mowing, or service in return for a certain number of signed-up referrals. But the challenge you have when giving away a free service is that it's something they would have had to pay for anyway. This means you are giving away a sale. For this reason I prefer to give away something they wouldn't usually buy from me.

What you need to make sure of is that your gifts have a low hard cost, and a perceived high cost. For instance, if I ran a lawn mowing business, I would offer a free cleanup of their garden when they next booked a mowing. I'd emphasize that I'd cart away and dispose of their garden refuse as well as any other junk they might have lying around at the same time—all at no cost to them. They would perceive this to have a high value as it would save them the trouble of hiring a trailer, loading it up, and driving to the nearest municipal dump to dispose of it. Yet to me the hard cost would be extremely low as I'd already have the trailer and would be making regular trips to the dump anyway. Charlie offers free car washes for every car serviced.

But let's get back to thinking about the dollar side of our business equation.

As you've already worked out how much you can afford to invest in acquiring each new customer, all you have to do once you've decided what gift you want to offer them is to add the cost of this gift into your equation.

Remember, the best gifts you can give anyone are those with a high perceived value yet little or no hard cost to you. There are many ways of ensuring this. For instance, Charlie once gave away a gift that introduced his customers to another business. You see, there was a new restaurant in his area that was desperate to establish itself. They were on the lookout for new customers. They were willing to offer a free meal to new customers, so this is where he came in. By offering his customers a free meal for every set number of referrals they brought him, he in turn referred them to the restaurant who paid for the free meal and added them to their customer base at the same time. But as far as Charlie's customers were concerned, it was Charlie who gave the free meal. This strategy works very well indeed.

Other examples are a men's clothing shop that gives out free ties, a car accessory shop that gives free car mats, a butcher that gives meat for a BBQ people have just bought, and so on. The possibilities are endless.

Giving gifts in exchange for referrals is really only limited by your imagination, but remember, you must test different gifts first because some work better than others. Some bring praise, some bring sales, and some bring both praise and sales.

Which will yours bring? Make notes now.

## MY *ACTION* STEPS ARE:

_____

_____

_____

_____

_____

_____

_____

## *Action* Strategy Number 14

> **Let your customers give their family, friends, and associates a gift from you.**

While allowing your customers to give out gifts on your behalf is a very powerful strategy, don't forget your customers themselves; give them a gift as well just for making a few referrals.

How does this work in practice? You see, you can't give them loads of gifts and hope they do the right thing; you need to retain control because it is, after all, your business we're talking about.

There are many ways you could do this, but here is what Charlie does:

- When a customer supplies him with a list of referrals, he contacts them individually and sends out the gift.

- When a customer gives him a list of referrals, he gives the customer a gift voucher for each referral on the list. He contacts the referrals and his customers hand out the gift vouchers.

The next question usually is: "What can I give away?" Here are a few ideas.

- A restaurant can give a free meal to friends of your customers. This works well because generally people tend not to eat on their own, preferring instead to eat out in the company of friends.

- An accountant can give away a free consultation.

- A clothing store can give away a piece of clothing.

- A home alarm company can give away a free smoke detector.

- Give away a redeemable voucher that your prospect can spend on anything you stock.

What you should be aiming at here is being proactive when dealing with future clients, putting in place marketing strategies that make them come in, giving you the opportunity to convert them into customers. This is best achieved by giving gifts that introduce you to them by allowing them to sample what you sell.

Here are a few general rules you need to follow:

- Be sure to make each voucher a great advertisement for your business.
- Your free gift must have a much greater perceived value than real hard cost.

When you are giving away a gift to a prospect, giving them a free service works really well. In fact, this is probably one of the best ways to greatly increase the size of your business.

You need to do your homework well before embarking on this strategy for a number of very good reasons. If you don't, it could cost you dearly.

So, what are these reasons, and why do you need to do your homework thoroughly?

Well, to start with, you need to find out what you can afford to give away. Once you have a rough idea of this, the next thing you need to do is to make sure your conversion rate is high enough for the whole exercise to be profitable. The basic idea here is, after all, to make you money while increasing the size of your business.

Once you have a good idea of the answers to these questions, you need to plan to give away as much as you can handle. Its no use flooding the market with free gifts and then having an avalanche of prospects calling in, totally overwhelming you and your team. This would be counterproductive and would only achieve the opposite of what you set out to achieve. You'd soon have a whole army of disgruntled people bad-mouthing you simply because you couldn't cope on the day.

My experience suggests that the biggest mistake people make here is poor follow-up, which leads directly to the loss of a great deal of potential sales.

What you need to remember is this: Only give away as much as you can realistically handle; otherwise the whole exercise will turn out to be very costly indeed.

Here's something else you should remember: The gifts you give to new prospects need to be very different than the ones you give to existing customers, because you still have to convert your new prospects by selling to them, whereas your existing customers already like doing business with you.

Over the years I have found that if you give credit to your customers for giving the gift, they'll want to sell more for you. Isn't that interesting and useful to know?

But be sure to follow these prospects up. Be sure too to test and measure your follow-ups and to always work with only the number of prospects you can handle at any one time. Don't make the common mistake of becoming greedy; it will get you nowhere and cost you plenty. And always remember to continually give great service.

## MY *ACTION* STEPS ARE:

_____

_____

_____

_____

_____

_____

_____

## *Action* Strategy Number 15

> **You can afford to give simple gifts both ways and possibly double the effectiveness of your strategy.**

Rather than just giving gifts to either your existing customers or their family and friends, here are some ideas on how you can combine them for greater results.

But before I discuss this, bear in mind that when you first start out along the referral-based business path, you probably won't need to go to these lengths. Concentrating on just your present customers will probably be more than enough to get your business buzzing.

As you read through each idea I'm about to discuss, bear in mind these three important points:

- How much can you afford to invest when buying new customers?

- What is your conversion rate?

- How many new prospects can you deal with at any one time?

Only when you know the answer to these three questions can you begin trying several of the following ways of buying new referrals.

- Charlie gives a gift to both his existing clients and the referrals he gets irrespective of what happens. You'd usually only use this strategy when you want to reward your existing customers anyway. The gift you'd give to the referrals will usually be small and designed to entice them into making a commitment of some kind to receive it. For example, you could give out a buy-one-get-one-free voucher.

- Charlie also gives his existing customers a gift based on the number of quality referrals they give him. When you know your conversion rate from new referral through to sale, you can afford to set a particular number of referrals for them to qualify for their gift.

- Charlie gives his existing customers a gift based on the number of sales he gets from their referrals. Generally you'd use this when you're giving away a big gift.

- Charlie gives his existing customers a gift for every sale that comes from someone they referred to him. Here I'd usually give gift checks that your customers can spend with you in the future, making each sale you get from one of their referrals worth a certain value.

If both gifts you give lead to extra sales or if they have a minimal hard cost and a high perceived value, then this will be one of the best strategies you can use to get referrals and, of course, extra sales for your business.

My advice is to test the gifts you give because some will give you a much larger list of referrals than others. Once you know this, then stick with the gift that works best.

Just remember to do the numbers before getting started. Remember too to follow up each referral you get. To neglect this last but vital step will make your entire strategy a complete waste of time. It'll be like letting gold slip between your fingers. Or, in rugby terms, it'll be like getting the ball, doing all the hard work in dodging opposition players and weaving your way across the field towards the try line, only to drop the ball just before you get there.

The follow-up is by far the easiest part of the whole exercise. You see, having come this far, your new prospect will be standing there full of anticipation and excitement. To close the sale and make a new customer, all you will usually have to do is simply ask for the sale. It really couldn't be easier.

## MY *ACTION* STEPS ARE:

_____

_____

_____

_____

_____

_____

_____

_____

## *Action* Strategy Number 16

**Mail out a referral card with all your orders, or just drop one in each shopping bag.**

When you decide to build a referral-based business, you should never miss a chance to ask people for new referrals.

As you go through life (and as your customers go through theirs) you get to meet a lot of people who could all be good referrals for any business you deal with. For this reason you should always be asking your customers for new referrals.

You also need to bear in mind that just because someone didn't give you a referral this month it doesn't mean they never will. This makes it even more important that you keep asking your existing clients for referrals. Make absolutely certain that a card goes to every customer you have on a regular basis. Make sure too that you give a card to customers when they make a purchase just in case they have someone new to refer to you.

I've been talking about cards here. What type of cards are they? How might they look?

Charlie makes use of three types of cards:

1. The first is a tear-off section on his business card. He makes his business card into a simple referral tool by having a second flap with a headline that says, *"You've been given this card by someone who thinks you're special."*

2. The second is a mail card that has his Reply Paid Address on it and a space on the back for his customer to refer two or three colleagues to him. This card is linked up with a gift that he sends each customer in exchange for having this card completed and sent in to him.

3. The third is a business-card-sized referral card that he gives liberally to customers. The idea here is for them to pass these on to their families and friends, telling them to make contact with Charlie's Garage. The beauty of this method is that it indicates an interest in what Charlie has to offer, if they do bring the cards back in.

Once you have all your cards printed, you'll no doubt be eager to start distributing them. But before you rush out and begin handing them to everyone in your shop, think for a minute; there might be a more cost-effective and efficient way of going about this. You see, you don't want to be wasting a large percentage of them as they do cost money to print, don't they?

Here are some ways you can get your cards directly to the people who may be more likely to pass them on and bring in the referrals you are after:

- Include a card in your regular newsletter that you send to customers.

- Contact another business and arrange to include your card in their newsletter.

- Slip a card in with your invoices.

- When sending out products ordered by customers, include a few referral cards.

- Have a pile of referral cards placed on your front counter with a sign asking customers to take some and hand them out.

- Get your checkout person to drop one in each shopping bag as customers pay for their purchases.

- Make arrangements with other businesses for them to include your cards with their next mailing of invoices.

Can you think of any more? Are there any other ways that are unique to your particular business or industry? I'm sure there are. The point is, once you've got your cards printed, it's a relatively easy matter to get them to those who can make good use of them.

So what are you waiting for? Have some cards printed; they'll certainly make getting referrals so much easier for you.

## MY *ACTION* STEPS ARE:

_____

_____

_____

_____

_____

_____

_____

## *Action* Strategy Number 17

**Put a sign or sticker on all of your products and make people an offer.**

Think of all the places your products end up. Think now about turning your products into advertisements in their own right so that they can bring you in new business. Charlie places a sticker onto the inside of each car's windshield after a service. Not only does this remind the driver when the next service is due (these details face inside), but it also advertises his garage because it has his logo and contact details on the side that faces out.

Just take the time to ask a few of your customers if you could include a small sign with each of your products that they have in their workplaces. If their customers see the signs, it can be a source of new business for you.

As marketing people would say, you'd be tapping into a new method to increase your marketing reach. You'd be reaching people who you might never ordinarily have been able to reach.

In fact, it might even be worth offering your client a small discount if they were to display your sign next to your product. Who knows what the results of this would be. It is definitely worth testing, if you have product that is distributed to customers who would make use of them in sight of their own customers.

Some of the businesses I have seen use this really successfully include a plant rental business (all rental businesses can use this, for that matter), telephone system companies, computer companies, glass repair companies, and security gate and fence companies. I have also been to restaurants where all the décor has signs indicating where similar items can be purchased.

If you are able to implement this strategy, make sure that everyone knows how to contact you if they want to. What's the point of successfully promoting your product to a new market, only to lose those leads because you didn't include clear contact details on your sign? Remember too to give these new potential prospects a good enough reason to make contact with you. People don't call in just because they saw your product; they need to know what's in it for them.

Getting your products increased exposure in this manner could take different forms like volunteering your products for use in the window displays of other businesses. But make sure the window displays are in areas where your target market is likely to see them.

If you can get agreement to place your product in a window display, the other thing you should pay attention to is that your message reaches potentially new as well as existing customers. This will help increase your returns and make the exercise even more effective.

Of course there are many other ways you could use to get your name or products up in other people's businesses. Can you think of any?

Here's a short list of possibilities that may apply to your situation.

- Give your customers a nicely framed award that can hang in a prominent place in their reception area.

- Hand out wall calendars, pens, and desk blotters that bear your company's name and contact details.

- What about issuing datebooks, T-shirts, and hats?

- Hang up a framed copy of your Customer Commitment Statement in a customer's reception area.

- Keep copies of your newsletter in other businesses reception areas like doctor's waiting rooms or auto repair shops.

Every one of these ideas is about having your business promoted in as many places as you possibly can. But remember, just including your business name and phone number on these promotional pieces is not enough. You must make use of a good headline and a compelling list of benefits that will entice people to call. And one other thing: make them an offer that they simply won't be able to refuse if they're in the market for one of your products.

## MY *ACTION* STEPS ARE:

_____

_____

_____

_____

_____

_____

_____

_____

## *Action* Strategy Number 18

**Present a seminar or information night for your existing customers and have them bring their friends along.**

A seminar can give you the perfect opportunity to introduce yourself to new prospects. Make use of them to demonstrate the latest innovations in your marketplace, to show people how they can increase their sales of your product range, or simply to increase their product knowledge.

Charlie holds regular open days when he invites his customers and their friends to visit his workshop. Each one revolves around an interesting topic like how to care for your car's bodywork, how to get more miles out of your tires, or how to change your own oil. He also holds sessions for women drivers that show them how to change a flat tire, how to check the oil and water, and how to carry out routine checks.

Many people are frightened by the whole notion of holding a seminar for their customers. They find standing up in front of an audience daunting. Some even find it intimidating.

Yet the truth is that once you overcome your initial fear, it's really quite simple. The first step to doing this is to understand just what fear is; once you know this, you'll begin to see seminars as the amazingly powerful marketing tools they really are.

So what then is fear? It is nothing more than *False Expectations Appearing Real*. It is nothing more than an illusion. And illusions are easily dealt with, aren't they? Of course they are. You see, if you allow fear to rule your life, you aren't in control of your destiny. And in a business sense, I'm sure you'll agree that if you allow fear to dictate what you do and what you don't, you'll be leading a very limited existence. This means your options will be limited by your fear, won't they?

So get over it, see it for what it really is, and do what you have to do to drive your business forward.

Remember that when you stand up in front of those who come to listen to what you have to say, they will be viewing you as the expert; they will see you as being in control. And they won't know what to expect, so don't be afraid that things might not go according to plan or that you'll forget in which order you must say things. They will be none the wiser and will not think to themselves, "Ah, he's messed that topic up because it should have come after the bit about X."

Just relax and think of seminars like a gathering of your friends. You are, after all, the expert in your field, aren't you? You do know more about what you will presenting than your audience does.

Here's another very powerful concept you need to bear in mind: by positioning yourself as the expert, you will become the person people will want to buy from.

Seminars are wonderful opportunities for you to teach people how to buy, what to buy, and why they should be buying from you. Done well they can provide your business with a rich source of qualified leads.

So how do you go about making sure you get the maximum rewards for your effort?

Here are some tips that will ensure your next seminar is a huge success.

- Go for quality at the seminar; don't compromise. Choose a good venue, a great speaker, nice refreshments, and provide great information.

- Be sure to invite between 5 and 10 times the number of people you want to attend.

- Make sure you fill your seminar room; choose a room that is just right for the audience you expect to turn up. It's better to have to put out extra chairs to accommodate everyone than having a room that's only half full.

- Give everyone name tags; use one color for your existing customers and another for new prospects.

- Give people plenty of opportunity to ask questions.

- Make sure people can buy from you that night; make them a great offer that's only available to those who attend.

- Ensure that your entire team is present and ready to talk to prospective customers.

- Follow up immediately.

If you are to do the speaking yourself, you must take advantage of the situation and make maximum use of all the opportunities your seminar will be presenting you. Don't just rely on what happens during the seminar itself; make use of the event to gain additional publicity for yourself. Invite your local newspaper or industry magazine to attend. If this isn't possible, then take some photos yourself and feature the seminar in your own newsletter.

When it comes to deciding on the format the event will take, make sure you structure it so that your attendees receive about 80 or 90 percent information and only 10 or 20 percent selling. The last thing you want them to feel is that you have conned them into attending so that you and your team can get down to some hard selling. People hate feeling pressured into anything, and particularly into buying something they may not actually need or want. If you fall into this trap, you will quickly get a bad reputation, and this will torpedo any future efforts you might make.

What you must be aiming at achieving through running seminars is to position yourself as the expert in your particular field, not the best salesperson. You see, my experience shows that people like to buy from experts, as they can be trusted.

So what can you do to make seminars work for you? Jot down your ideas now.

## MY *ACTION* STEPS ARE:

_____

_____

_____

_____

_____

_____

_____

## *Action* Strategy Number 19

**Encourage your customers to buy gift vouchers to introduce their friends.**

If you knew that every time you sold a gift voucher you were introducing another brand new lifelong customer to your business, what else would you do to sell more gift vouchers?

This is a very interesting question, isn't it? But before we discuss it in any great detail, ask yourself these two questions:

1. Do *all* your customers know that you sell gift vouchers?

2. Do they use them?

If you are like most businesses, the answer to both will most probably be *no*.

So what do you do about it? How do you get them excited enough to actually make use of them? This is what Charlie does:

He promotes them wherever he can—in his newsletters, in his advertisements, with signs in his garage, and by slipping a message in with his accounts. His aim is to ensure all his customers know they can buy gift vouchers from him.

The great thing about gift vouchers is that people will generally buy something totaling more than the value of the gift voucher, and if they do they will be more than willing to chip in the difference. This will be the easiest piece of up-selling you'll ever do, so don't discount gift vouchers as an important and lucrative strategy. The other great thing about them is they will get your new customers to come back time and again if you take good care of them during their initial visit. You see, they will be in a good frame of mind when they first come in because the purpose of their visit will be to spend their gift vouchers. How you treat them during that visit will determine whether or not you have a potential lifelong customer.

OK, so how could you go about introducing gift vouchers if you don't have them at present?

This is where you get to have a lot of fun. Why not give each of your existing customers a free $5 gift voucher together with a letter explaining that you have just introduced them and you wanted them to be the first to know about them. You could go on to encourage them to buy gift vouchers for their family and friends instead of the usual birthday or Christmas presents.

Then, once you've had your gift vouchers printed, personally endorse each one for a certain dollar amount. This way you won't be stuck with a few preprinted amounts like $10, $50, and $100. A customer could buy one for $18.50 if that's what they want.

This makes them perfect to use for different promotional activities. For example, if you were to notice a new prospect come into your store, browse around, and make for the door again without making a purchase, why not walk up and hand over an envelope that contains a letter and a $5 gift voucher. On the outside of the letter is printed, *don't open this until you get home."*

They would be tempted to open it right away, wouldn't they?

You could also mail out a $5 gift voucher to customers who do make a purchase. The accompanying note would say, "Thanks for making a purchase. Here's a little incentive to come back sometime."

How do you think that person would feel on opening the envelope? Pretty good, huh?

You can use the vouchers as flyers that give people $5 as long as they spend $25 with you.

There are literally hundreds of uses for gift vouchers and dozens of ways to use them to bring you new customers. Can you think of any more that might give you the edge over your competitors?

How about these? Send four or five $5 gift vouchers to each of your past customers. On each have the customer's name printed at the top, with "A Gift to You From . . ." underneath. Now when each customer hands this to a friend, and the friend comes in and makes a purchase, you will know who referred the new customer, so send that person a small gift in appreciation.

The list of things you could do to encourage referrals through gift vouchers is endless. It's also a lot of fun. If you promote this strategy properly, you could easily get a real buzz going in your business, with customers running around referring people, and those referrals then becoming customers just to get their own gift vouchers to hand on to their friends, and so continues the cycle.

Can you see how this strategy can create Raving Fans as well as new customers? It can be very powerful. Is there a place for it in your business? What can you do to sell more gift vouchers? Put down your ideas now.

## MY *ACTION* STEPS ARE:

_____

_____

_____

_____

_____

_____

_____

## *Action* Strategy Number 20

> **Introduce yourself to a whole new market with a bring-a-friend sale.**

If you have to hold a sale—for instance if you have to reduce stock—it's best to pass on the benefits to your existing customers, and while you're doing so, be sure to have them bring a friend along to get the same benefits.

This is a really great strategy that works very well indeed. But before I go into detail, let me first introduce you to the concept of a closed-door sale.

I'm going to give you a broad overview of a particular type of sale that really produces results.

There are four main things to consider:

### Invitation Letter

Your invitation letter should create real excitement and make people want to cancel whatever plans they had to come to your sale.

### Offers

If you're not offering people a real incentive to come, it's unlikely they will. Your offers (or specials) need to be truly enticing. It's common to have a number of "loss leaders" to get people in the door—these are items you sell well below cost.

### Customer Service

If your team just stands around at the sale, looking disappointed because they're missing *Melrose Place* on television, people will be unlikely to really spend. You need to greet people warmly, help them find what they're looking for, then really make an effort to sell them something else as well.

### Social Occasion

The best closed-door sales are the ones that turn into a miniparty. People come with friends, stay around to eat your snacks, and walk out with an armful of purchases. Of course, not every business will have the opportunity to create this vibe, but it's something to aim for. Just think of it like this: You're inviting hundreds of friends over. How are you going to give them a good time and make sure they stay?

You'll find that running a successful closed-door sale is as easy as following a well-established formula. If you want to go into this is greater detail, read my book *Instant Repeat Business.*

One of the greatest benefits of closed-door sales is to get quality referrals, and lots of them. You invite all your customers and make the price of entry to the sale one friend who has never bought from your business before. That's right, if people want to come along and check out the awesome specials and bargains, they have to bring a friend along. Not only will the friend probably buy something, boosting your takings for the night, there's a good chance they'll become a regular customer as well, especially if they enjoy themselves and like the stock you offer. Often, you'll hear your customer's friends say, "I normally go to [one of your competitors], but they never have anything like this." That's precisely the kind of response you want to elicit. The friends start to believe they've been missing out.

Now that you have a general idea of what a closed-door sale is, it's time to consider how you get people to come along. This is very easy. Simply write a letter to your customers telling them about this day where they'll actually need to produce their invitation and a friend to get into your store. Tell them about some of the great bargains they could have and reassure them this opportunity is restricted to special customers only.

Once you've done that, you need to set aside an appropriate day for the event. Cover your windows so nobody can see in, put a security guard on the front door, and arrange some drinks and snacks on a table somewhere inside the store.

What you'll be doing is closing the entire store to everyone except your special customers and their invited guests. Make sure to leave a space on the invitations for guests to fill in their names, addresses, and other contact details; this will allow you to adopt a proactive approach to your follow-ups soon after.

Another way to make sure this works is to give everyone who attends a gift. Do this whether they buy or not. This strategy will ensure you get massive numbers attending, and if you consider them all as prospects, the only real cost to you for each will be the price of the gift you give.

Another way to ensure your event is a huge success is to give even better sale prices to those who bring more than one friend. You could also have a sliding scale, which allows for a bigger range of discounts depending on how many people they bring along.

You could keep it simple and let everyone know that they only qualify for the sale price if they bring along a friend.

The list of possibilities is endless; you could combine some of these ideas, for instance offering a gift collection to those who bring along one or more friends.

Now I know some of you will be thinking: "This is all very well and good, but my business isn't a store. We don't do business this way. We are not a retail outfit."

That's fine. There are many businesses like this, and they can all still utilize this strategy. If you are one of these, then it's time to get a little creative. It's time to adapt this strategy so that you too can reap some of the amazing benefits from it like so many other businesses have.

Here are a few ideas that Charlie uses. They might also stimulate your thinking so that you can come up with a unique variation. If they do, then write them down in the table below.

He holds regular closed-door sales by fax. He faxes out details of what's on sale (and the extra special prices available to only good customers who introduce a friend) and include a "friend only" fax order form. This form includes his customer's name on it so he knows who made the referral when the order comes in.

Because he has a membership card system in his business, he gives his customers "honorary membership cards" for them to pass on to their friends. He cross-references each with a variation of the original's membership number so that he can trace back to the one doing the referring.

He also holds a friends-only open day. He opens the doors to his workshop and shows these new prospects around. Of course, he gives them extra special incentive to become customers while they are there.

As you can see, this strategy is so versatile you can adapt it, change it, or re-invent it as many times as you like, without altering the basic results you'll get. How can you use it right now? Can you think of any unique variations that will attract prospects like you haven't had before?

## MY *ACTION* STEPS ARE:

## *Action* Strategy Number 21

> **Throw a party to celebrate your customers' purchases and invite their friends along.**

Imagine the scene: Charlie has just finished a complete rebuild of a classic sports car for a long-time customer, who is beside himself with excitement. Then, as he is handing over the keys, he tells his customer that he'd like to throw a party for him to celebrate the completion of the car. The delighted customer looks surprised and a little dubious. Charlie reassures him it won't cost him anything, as he will be supplying all the food and drinks.

The size of the customer's smile increases. All he need do, Charlie explains, is to give him a list of his car club friends' names and addresses and he'll do the rest.

Once the customer has done this, the next thing Charlie does is to send an invitation, on his garage's letterhead, to the people on the list, inviting them to the party he's throwing. He explains in the letter that the reason for the party is to help the customer show off his newly restored sports car.

Each person on this invitation list is also entered onto Charlie's prospect database at the same time.

On the day of the party, Charlie turns up halfway through to drop off some extra drinks. Just think of the stir that causes!

So, what does this whole affair cost him? Typically, the total costs are in the region of $500. That's a really cost-effective way of getting a large group of good prospects together who will all be talking about Charlie's Garage and the great job he has just done on their friend's pride and joy.

There are variations to this theme as well. For instance, if you are in the business of selling cars, you could host a BBQ for everyone who bought from you that month. The proviso would be, of course, that each person had to bring a friend along.

But it's not just "high ticket" items that can benefit from this strategy. If you sell cheaper products, you could run cocktail referral parties for your customers, who would once again be invited to bring along some friends.

If you use a powerful strategy like this, your customers will love you. They will also love the idea of being able to bring their friends along. But you do need to stipulate the type of person you want them to invite. If you do this well, you should be rewarded with a lot of sales from the event.

The secret to using a party to bring in referrals is to make sure you send out the invitations on behalf of your customers, and that you do this as close to when they made the purchase as you possibly can.

The key to the success of this strategy is understanding that your customers' friends will generally be in roughly the same position or stage of life as they are, and any way you can find to celebrate their successes by including their friends will generally result in more sales for you. All it takes is a little imagination, some courage to do things a little differently, and a determination to have some fun.

Never lose sight of the fact that your customers have a whole lot of friends who are just as willing as they are to buy. All you need to do is to find a way of reaching them. And what better way than through a party? So, what can you do to become the talk of the town?

**MY *ACTION* STEPS ARE:**

_____

_____

_____

_____

_____

_____

_____

_____

$$\boxed{\textbf{Part 6}}$$

# ■ A Real-Life Example

It's now time to take a look at a real business so that you can get an idea of just how powerful some of these referral strategies can be. You see, it's all very well reading the theory and understanding how these strategies *should* work, *why* they should, and *what* the likely results could be, but there's probably still this question lingering somewhere in the back of your mind: "Hey, but do they work *in the real world*?"

This is the million-dollar question, and it's a very valid one. You see, as the old saying goes, the proof of the pudding is in the eating.

So, are there any good examples I could use to demonstrate this? Of course there are. There are literally thousands that my coaches and I have been involved with over the years, but because of space limitations I've chosen one real-life example to talk about here.

I like to use real-life examples to explain what I'm talking about because:

- They demonstrate the theory in a real-world setting.

- They put things in context.

- They illustrate very well that businesses really start to fly when a mix of strategies are implemented simultaneously.

- They show that nothing is perfect.

- They show that, with a little bit of help and accountability, business owners can exceed their wildest expectations.

I also like to use real-life examples that show what happened "warts and all." You see, I believe in telling it like it is (with the owner's permission, of course) so that it's *believable*. This is why I publish *all* the details of the business I'm using in my examples.

OK, let's turn our attention to this business, which is a men's clothing shop situated in Sydney, Australia.

Now remember the basic aim of all businesses is to generate a profit for its owners and/or shareholders. Agree? Good. Let's push on.

Let's assume for a moment that you own that shop. Let's also assume that it's the beginning of the year (calendar or financial, it doesn't really matter) and that one of the aims you've set is to increase your profits this year compared to last.

How much would you say is reasonable to aim for? What would your accountant say is reasonable if you were to ask? Five percent? What about 10 percent?

Come on, try it. Don't just sit there passively reading these few paragraphs. Think about it for a moment. Do you think you'd have a reasonable chance of succeeding if you were to aim for a 20 percent increase in profits this year?

Well, what if I were to challenge you to aim for 600 percent? Would you think that achievable?

Would a figure of that magnitude surprise you? Well if it does, it shouldn't. You see, this is the type of increase I'm talking about. This is the type of result you could achieve in your business through the implementation of some of these powerful strategies.

But that's not all you'll achieve, either. You'll probably get to work a *whole lot less*. Don't believe me? Well then, read on. It's time to introduce you to Tim and Natasha Roberts, who own The Club Shoppe. You'll also meet Greg Albert, one of my Coaches.

## The Business

**Name:**              The Club Shoppe

**Address:**           Shop 47–48 St. Ives Shopping Village, St. Ives NSW, Australia

**Director/Owner:** Tim and Natasha Roberts

**Business Sector:** Retail, Menswear

**Purchased:**        1999

**Coach:**             Greg Albert

## The Challenge

When Tim and Natasha bought their business, they set themselves a few goals that they thought were reasonable. They wanted to make the business profitable, and to increase turnover by 50 percent and profit by 70 percent. To put this in perspective, they thought that if they could make a total profit of $150,000, they'd be more than happy. They also wanted to pay $150,000 on their business loan and to be in a position to hire a new team member.

Of course, they also set themselves some personal goals such as being able to spend more time with the family, to earn enough to landscape the backyard, and to get focus and direction back into their lives.

So, how did they feel on purchasing the business? Instead of feeling elated, they felt lost, and instead of feeling self-satisfied, they felt trapped—hardly what they expected on achieving their dream of owning their own business.

To make matters worse, the business had a severe cashflow problem when they bought it. It had too much inventory tied up. Profitability was low and discounting normal.

Like many new business owners, they decided to keep the original owner on in an effort to make a smooth transition, feeling reluctant to try anything new. There was no loyalty program in place and no real communication with clients. It soon became blatantly obvious to them that their best marketing efforts had not worked.

It was not a fun place to be, and the atmosphere could be described as dull, at best. They spent their days just waiting for clients to walk in.

Now that you have a basic understanding of the situation facing Tim and Natasha, let's hear the details from Tim. This will give you a very good understanding of what he went through in facing up to the challenges that lay before them. It will also give you an idea of how important it is to take responsibility for your situation, in being able to recognize the signs, and to take positive steps to put things back on track, so you can meet your longer-term goals.

## Tim's Story

When I left school in 1989, I never in my wildest dreams thought I would end up in retail, let alone owning a business that sells menswear. In fact, before I bought The Club Shoppe in 1999, I knew absolutely nothing about menswear.

I actually started out as a school teacher and although it's a noble profession, I discovered real early that it was not for me, and that it would not take me to where I wanted to go.

So with the help of my family, I decided to buy a business. In fact, it was a small music store that just happened to be situated next door to the menswear store that I would eventually buy. I was relatively successful with my music store, but had developed a passion for menswear, so I decided to go for it.

It would also be fair to say that prior to meeting my Business Coach, Greg Albert, in 2001, I knew very little about how to run a business effectively and profitably, although I never realized that at the time. In the 14 months that I followed Greg's lead, I have turned The Club Shoppe into a viable and profitable business that is now a lot of fun, an integral part of my life, and a business with huge potential.

But I'm jumping ahead here. Let me start at the beginning.

The Club Shoppe was established in 1959 by the then Minister for the Environment, the Honorable Mr. Barry Cohen. Soon thereafter, Barry employed Ray Jacomb to manage the business while he pursued his political ambitions.

In the 35 years that followed, Ray turned The Club Shoppe into one of the best menswear stores in the country, selling only the finest clothing available anywhere in the world.

When I bought the business, The Club Shoppe was operating just as it always had—very smoothly and generating good profit, or so I thought.

The shop is based on the north side of Sydney in an affluent suburb, and stocks the very top-end of men's fashion.

When I bought the business, I knew nothing about menswear. I didn't even know how to read a tape measure. However, I had an extremely good mentor in

Ray, who, fortunately for me, had decided to stay on for another two years to teach me every aspect of the business.

I dedicated myself to learning the basics during the first 12 months. I was so determined to learn the business that I could not think of anything else. I lived and breathed the business, everything from how to sell a suit to ordering clothing for the new season. I literally drained Ray of information. You see, I was thirsty for information, and he was more than happy to give it to me.

After the first 12 months, however, I began to realize the business had a lot of flaws, and I noted that they were very serious flaws.

These included the following:

- At the beginning of every season, the business experienced very severe cashflow problems, which were impacted by the introduction of the Goods and Services Tax. These problems arose from trying to find the cash for the duty, freight, and Goods and Services Tax on imported goods. Every season this amounted to over $100,000, and it always materialized during the quietest times of the year (that is at the beginning of a season). Although we were making good profit, all of it was tied up in excess stock.

- Because The Club Shoppe was established in 1959, it had a very dedicated clientele. The problem was they were getting older. Many of the customers whom the shop was built around were retiring and no longer needed the expensive suits or a new range of casual clothing every season. I could see that for 10 or so years the shop's turnover was stagnant and did not rise or fall by more than 30,000 or 40,000 every year. I was worried that in 10 years, I would not have a business left.

- For 40 years, the shop had been built around Ray, who would work more than 50 hours a week. Customers would come into the store looking for him and some would only come back when he was there. I was absolutely petrified of what would happen to the business when he decided to retire. Even though I had learned extremely quickly and knew I could do everything he could, people still wanted Ray to look after them.

- The shop had developed something of a discount culture; we regularly gave discounts to our VIPs and we had numerous sales, which tended to attract the wrong type of customer—price shoppers—so our profitability was heading in the wrong direction.

- Although I did not know it at the time, I had become reliant on the "old ways" of doing business. For the first 15 months I had a bookkeeper who looked after everything from paying bills to doing the banking. She was also, you might say, my own secretary. This was a big mistake. Although this bookkeeper did her work well, I never had a handle on the company's finances. I never knew the impact my cashflow problems were having on the business. I didn't even know how much I owed suppliers or how much I had in the bank at any one time. I realize now how silly I was at that time, but in hindsight, I was spending all my time in the shop concentrating on the physical aspects of selling.

After the first 12 months, the excitement of a new business was truly wearing off. The GST had been implemented and the Sydney Olympic Games were looming. Business was down, cashflow was pathetic, and I felt absolutely trapped. What's more, my wife Natasha had just delivered our first child and her maternity leave was about to run out. We had two choices: Either she would go back to work, or I'd have to build a place for her in the business. We chose the latter.

Natasha took charge of computerizing all our accounts in the business. This turned out to be the first of many steps we took to turn the business around. And it was the first time that I could see every dollar being spent, and earned. I started to gain control of the business, and I really started to feel that it was mine. Our current bookkeeper decided to leave, and this gave Natasha and me real scope as far as the accounts were concerned. I could see that we were ordering too much stock. I also realized we had far too many suppliers.

Things began to improve, and by the end of that financial year, we actually made a nice little profit. I put this solely down to the fact that we had better financial management. However, I still felt trapped. I wanted to spend more time with my family, yet I felt tied to the shop. I was constantly under pressure to be there more.

## The Moment of Truth

It all changed one fateful night in September, 2001. The management of the shopping center had invited a representative from *Action International* to do a free seminar on sales and marketing to show us how we could improve our businesses. I thought I would go along just to see what these "consultants" were all about and what ideas they might have.

I thought it was all very weird when one of their representatives started trying to balance about 10 helium balloons all at once. I was actually going to get up and leave.

Then it all changed. Greg Albert stood up and started to pull my strings. He asked the group how many of us were truly free of our businesses. How many of us could take days, weeks, or months off whenever we wanted to. How many of us could be assured our businesses would run efficiently and effectively whether we were working or not. How many of us truly valued the concept of time, and how many of us were spending our time doing things we enjoyed, or would rather be doing something else.

Greg proceeded to tell us all about *Action International* and the options that were available in their *Action* Plan. I took the information home and told Natasha about my evening. I remember going to sleep thinking, "I dare you to give it a try."

The very next day I did.

I gave Greg a call and the rest, for me, is history.

During my first meeting with Greg, he asked, "What is it that you want most of all from your business?" At that stage my sights were limited. I knew Natasha wanted our backyard landscaped, so I replied, "I want the business to earn enough money so we could get our backyard landscaped."

Greg smiled wryly and asked, "OK, so we are in September, what do you want from the business in October?"

I'd never really thought about it before, but Greg kept asking questions, delving deeper and deeper. It all really came down to one thing: time. I began to realize this was the commodity I wanted most.

I wanted to spend time with my family—time to do whatever I wanted, when I wanted. I didn't want to feel trapped and full of worry.

I'm sure you have all heard the saying, "Spend more time working *on* the business, not *in* it." I never really understood that until I started working with

Greg. For the first three months, that's what Greg taught me to do. I systemized everything in the business, from opening up the shop, to how to measure up a client for a suit, to how to manage the computerized Point-of-Sale System. This seemed at the time an extremely tiresome job, however I absolutely loved it. I could see that it was the first step toward building a better business.

It wasn't long before I could afford to spend a day at home each week working on the business. This totally reenergized me and I began to think, "Hey, this can really work for me."

Greg taught me that consistency was the key to a successful business. It was also the key to releasing myself from working *in* the business and spending more time working *on* the business. You see, if a customer were to come into the shop, she must experience the same level of service no matter who served her. And she must have exactly the same experience every time she comes in.

This was my first step to making the business less reliant on Ray, and also on me.

We started a VIP program and set about signing up our key A-grade clients. We then began holding special events every month. But what we needed most, at the time, was to make some quick cash.

In October of 2001, I had my first taste of a successful marketing campaign, and what an absolute eye-opener that was. Once we had our new stock in for that season, we experienced our first success. Greg suggested we hold a closed-door sale for my loyal customers. So I invited them to an event to celebrate the arrival of our new season's stock. We served refreshments and gave anyone who spent in excess of $1500 a dinner at one of Sydney's most exclusive Italian restaurants.

I must admit that I did have certain expectations and hoped for a good turnout, but never in my wildest dreams did I think I'd get the turnout we did.

In one weekend we took in more than what we typically would in 10 days of trading. After the event, Ray said, "In my 37 years in this business, I have never, ever experienced anything quite like it!" What was even better was the fact that our takings were on full margin; there were no discounts given and nothing was "on sale." That day we gave out 13 dinners valuing $150 each.

I had started. I was now really hungry for more.

All of a sudden, instead of just plodding along and wishing for customers to come through the door, I proactively went after them. I started a frequent buyer's program that rewarded customers every time they bought, with points that could be redeemed at a later stage for goods from the shop.

I began to compile specific customer lists that grouped people together according to their likes and dislikes. This enabled me to plan promotions for each individual group and to make contact with each group specifically. For example, I organized a "Made-to-Measure" suit and jacket promotion and was able to reach my target market because I had a list of people who had an interest in "Made-to-Measure" articles. When we received new merchandise from particular labels such as Polo Ralph Lauren, I had a list of people who I knew wanted to be told about it.

I organized an agreement with Lavazza Coffee whereby I would serve their coffee to our customers if they supplied me the coffee and an espresso machine free of charge. I also had wine and whiskey for those customers who had had a particularly difficult day at work. And do you know what? Some customers began coming in just to say hello and to have a cup of tea. It was great.

I even recently invited the local Harley Davidson dealer to put a bike on display in the shop. It was great to see these "shopped-out" husbands dragging their wives into the store to see the Harley, and to hear their wives say, "Yeah, sure, but you need some new clothes!" Work was becoming really fun.

Greg warned me that other shop owners would think I was a bit weird. I remember once when shopping center traffic was slow, the other shop owners were complaining how slow business was. I was booming. They kept asking me how I did it, and I always said, "Get a coach." It amazed me that no one took my advice.

In the first six months of working with Greg, our turnover increased by 18 percent, but more importantly, our profit increased by nearly 40 percent. I was hooked. I have never enjoyed working so much.

When it came time for our next season's launch, I wanted to try something a little different. However, I didn't know what. One day I was speaking to Greg about the latest James Bond movie and he said, "Wouldn't it be great if we could get James Bond into the store for the promotion?"

Well, unfortunately Pierce Brosnan was busy that weekend, but I arranged for an Aston Martin DB7 to be on display in the shop instead. I also organized complimentary dinners at the MG Garage Restaurant for our customers. Well, that promotion was even more successful than the first.

What I really enjoyed most of all was hearing compliments from our customers like, "There is no other store that offers me as much as what you do," and, "You know you are ruining my overseas shopping experiences, because I just come here for everything now." Then there was this: "My husband keeps telling me to ask you to stop having promotions, because he enjoys coming here for them and always spends too much money."

I love these comments. It makes me think I'm doing something right. I mean I love communicating with my customers, and if they leave feeling happy, then I know I have done something right.

We basically changed the business from being a passive one (waiting for customers to turn up) to one that is a real fun place, one that is an incredible experience. This concept is breathtakingly simple, yet difficult for owners who are store-blind to see.

Go the extra mile. That is what Greg keeps telling me. We do things that I can guarantee nobody else does, like sending new customers thank-you gifts for coming into our shop, whether they buy anything or not. Or sending our good customers gifts like pen sets or calculators.

I remember one instance when a lady came into our store and began looking around. I introduced myself and struck up a conversation. She had never been into our store before, even though she was a local. She told me that her husband shopped at one our competitors about 20 kilometers away. I took her address and her husband's name. When she left, I boxed up a pen and pencil set that we had purchased for our good customers and promptly sent it to her. That weekend she and her husband came into the shop and spent over $6000. They are now dedicated customers.

"If you have to make a decision, make it in favor of the customer," Greg would say to the team. My team was becoming so good, it did not matter who served our customers. What a change.

I was able to promote my young salesperson to general manager. I then recruited another team member to train, Ray was able to semiretire, and I got to spend time with my family; we were all progressing towards realizing our own dreams.

One of the advantages of having a more successful business was that I managed to afford to increase the size of our store by 30 square meters, and I spent $50,000 fitting it out. Needless to say during the refit (funny how it always seems to take longer than expected), our turnover was not good. Consequently I decided to get in some ties for a promotion. Once the refit was completed, I sent out a letter to all our customers offering them a free tie just for coming to have a look at the new shop. Over a three-day period I gave away 23 ties (at the value of $11 each) and I took in over $23,000.

I still have a very long way to go in the business. In fact, I feel I have only just begun. My next step is to build the business to a stage where I could franchise it to begin making some passive income.

I am currently not only enjoying working in my business, but I also absolutely love the extra time I have with my young family. If that's all I ever achieve in life, then my time with Greg has been worthwhile.

I have gone from a position of negative cashflow, negative profits, working long hours, and questionable customer loyalty, to owning a company that is thriving.

Oh, and Greg managed to get our backyard makeover money in one weekend! I am so glad I got into *Action*!

## The Coach's Story

At first, Tim was very skeptical. However, he was in such a situation that he was willing to give business coaching a go. To begin with, he found the initial telephone coaching call not as effective as a face-to-face meeting (he's a real people person) but soon realized that it was more focused and productive.

Tim's a great client. He's very eager to learn and has an open mind and a desire to do whatever it takes. No matter how arduous the task or weird the suggestion, he would grab it with both hands and give it a go.

Tim's core values are aligned with those of *Action,* especially concerning rewarding customers and the team. Consequently, all strategies were painlessly implemented.

I started with an Alignment Consultation to get real clear on the goals and challenges. I then got him to read several books while an *Action* Plan was being prepared.

I started with the basics. This included preparing a cashflow forecast and developing a plan of action to swing this into positive territory. We then increased prices, stopped all discounting, and reduced costs, including the inventory. We negotiated better terms with suppliers. A team incentive plan was instituted. Simple routines were systemized. We measured various business activities and taught sales skills. Conversion rates (from prospects to clients) were monitored and measured. Scripts were introduced. We then established exclusive lines, created package deals, started a VIP program, and established events that we marketed to our VIPs every month. The first was a highly successful closed-door sale. We ran an off-premises old stock clearance, and set up numerous strategic alliances. Critical nonessentials were introduced. I then began training the team to build Raving Fans and introduced programs to keep customers for life. A new recruitment system for new team members was also introduced.

I'm pleased to report that the owner is now able to spend one full day a week working *on* the business (developing strategies, etc.) and has prepared clear budgets and targets, both monthly and weekly, that the team is monitored against.

## The Outcome

After three months, the owner was spending one day a week less at work. He reevaluated the team and introduced testing and measuring, as well as sales training. Their conversion rate increased from 50 percent to 70 percent. Discounting is now a thing of the past. Prices have actually been increased, and profit has gone from negative to +11 percent.

After six months, cashflow forecasts indicated an inventory challenge. This was tackled with new contracts put in place and "dead" stock cleared. The conversion rate was now better than 80 percent. A 10 percent increase in profit per month became our target. A new key team member was employed when an existing salesperson was promoted to general manager, freeing up the owner. Five hundred people were enrolled in the VIP program. They then secured the distribution rights for Brioni and Paul Smith suits, and introduced Made-to-Measure in Milan and Zegna suits. Turnover increased by 10 percent, with profit up 40 percent.

After 12 months the owner is able to go on vacation whenever he wants to. The business now services only A-grade clients and does not cater to price-shoppers or discount hunters at all. The store has a fun, happy, and professional atmosphere. A rental business is ready to launch. Turnover is up by 12 percent, and profit up by 600 percent. The business is now cashflow positive. Business systems are in place and the owner is looking at multiple outlets.

Isn't that a terrific story from the store owner and coach? You bet it is, but the good news is that it isn't unique. My coaches all over the world tell stories just like this.

Now what about you? Do you want your business to really fly, or are you quite content to continue on like you have been up until now? The choice is yours.

# ▌Testing and Measuring

You may have noticed that I'm big on testing and measuring. I have mentioned it in various places in this book and for good reason. If you are new to this vital business activity or if you doubt its value, then this section is directed specifically to you.

So before I discuss how to go about testing and measuring, let's first consider in more detail the reasons I believe it to be so important.

## Why Test and Measure?

If you don't know where your customers come from, you're really stabbing around in the dark. You'll have no real idea which referral campaigns are working, how well your salespeople are doing, or even how much each sale is "costing" you.

Once you know these things, you'll have the power to make decisions, and good ones at that. You'll know which referral campaigns to kill, which to improve, and which to spend more money on.

You'll also know where your key leverage point is—that is, the thing that you most need to improve. Perhaps your conversion rate is high but your leads are few, or maybe it's the other way around. Maybe you're doing well in both lead generation and conversion, but you're not selling enough high-priced items.

Once you know which area needs work, you can start to make some new, well-informed marketing decisions.

At the end of this section I've included a testing and measuring sheet designed for a general business, but if yours is a bit more specific, feel free to make the necessary changes.

## The Three Most Important Things about Testing and Measuring

1. Testing and measuring is nothing new. You've probably been doing it all your business life. Remember the newspaper advertising you tried that didn't work, and the radio spots that did? That's all testing is. It's about

finding out what produces results and what doesn't, then making decisions based on that.

2. You *must* start asking people where they found out about you. If you don't, you'll be operating in the dark forever. You may keep running a particular referral strategy that never brings in a sale, or you may accidentally kill a good one that brings in heaps. Customers usually come from so many sources it's impossible to judge how a particular strategy is working based on sales alone. Perhaps there was a festival in town and this brought you new business. Every time someone buys, ask this question: "By the way, can I just ask where you heard about my business?" No one, and I mean no one, will have any problem telling you.

3. Be vigilant and disciplined. You can't test and measure half the time; you must do it every hour of every day. It's not difficult. Just remember to make a record of it after every customer interaction. And make sure your employees do the same. Stress the importance of it and absolutely *demand* that they do. Also, tell them it's essential that they are honest.

## What to Do with Your Results

The first thing to do is to see what's not working. If a particular strategy is getting a very low response (which means the profit margin from the sales is not at least paying for the strategy), then kill it.

Of course, you need to consider the lifetime value of the customer as well. If, after taking all the factors into account, you're not getting the results you want, then bite the bullet and stop running it. You see, every time you run strategies that don't work, you're literally giving away money.

Now, you have two options: Channel your marketing funds elsewhere (like back into your pocket) or improve the strategy.

If you choose option two, there are a couple of things you can do to make the task simpler. First, go back over your past campaigns and think about how well each one worked. Pull out the best couple and see if you can pick what gave them their edge. Next, read a couple of books on marketing, or at least flip through them. Last, look at what your competitors are doing. Are they doing anything (that you are aware of, at least) that you should also be doing? Unless they're stupid, their campaigns must be doing OK. What ideas can you borrow from them?

Then develop a new campaign. Don't do anything with it yet—we'll get to that in a minute.

Go through this process with each strategy that doesn't seem to be working. By this I mean examine each element, what you are doing, how it's been executed, and so on.

Kill, examine, modify. Kill, examine, modify. Once you have a collection of revised ideas, just sit on them. There's something more important we need to deal with first, and that's the strategies that are working.

Run through each of the working strategies in depth, examining why they are producing results that the others aren't. See if you can pick the one important, attractive point about each. This in itself will teach you an incredible amount about your business.

Next, think of a way to do each strategy on a larger scale. If it's referral cards you're looking at, the answer is simple—deliver twice as many. That should bring twice the sales. If it's a seminar, run it more often, or increase its size. If it's gift vouchers, promote them harder.

But whatever you do, don't meddle. Just do the same thing on a larger scale.

After that, test and measure for another two weeks. Notice if the number of referrals remains the same or goes down. Also compare this with how much you're spending on marketing.

You'll probably find you barely miss those dud strategies and the "larger-scale" working strategies are paying off nicely. If it's not, return to the original.

Conversion is the number of referrals that become sales. You may find you get 1 in 10, 99 out of 100, or anything in between.

Leave it for a month or so and work on converting the referrals you have. A better conversion technique, plus more referrals from bigger-scale successful referral strategies, should give your business a boost.

The lack of dead money being poured into strategies that don't work should also give you a helping hand.

After running through this process, it's time to pull your revised "dud" strategies out of the drawer and give them a run.

Do one at a time, and track the result meticulously. Note exactly how many referrals it brings you, and how many of those turn into sales. Compare that with the marketing cost, and judge whether the strategy has been good.

If so, add it to your list of ongoing strategies. If not, don't give up hope. Try it again, testing a different approach, scale, or angle. Change a meaningful part and measure the results. If it doesn't work again, give it one more try. If you get the feeling *nothing* is going to work, abandon the idea, as it's probably the wrong approach altogether, and concentrate your efforts somewhere else.

Very soon, you'll develop a collection of referral strategies that work. Now that's a business success formula, and the real benefit of testing and measuring.

## How to Use the Daily Testing and Measuring Sheet

This sheet is ideal for most types of businesses, especially those with mid- to high-priced items. Give each member of your team a testing and measuring sheet. Total all sheets up at the end of the day, and then do a weekly total. Add these up to form your monthly total. Once you've done this, examine the sheets to determine which strategies have been working.

> **Prospect's Name:** The name of the customer. You need to ask him for it. If you don't get a chance to get his name, simply write a basic description of him, such as "Male 30s."

> **Repeat Customer (New Inquiry):** Tick this column if the customer is an old one, yet he has come in to discuss a new purchase. By this I mean one he hasn't previously talked to you about. It may be a product he's bought before—just as long as this is the first time you've talked to him about buying it this time around.

> **Repeat Customer (Same Inquiry):** Tick this column if the customer is an old customer and you have discussed the product or service before. That

means you have talked to her about the specific purchase she is considering making.

**New Customers (How Did They Hear about You?):** Fill this out if the customer is entirely new. That is, he has never been in before. Ask him where he heard about you. Don't suggest anything if he takes a while to answer—wait for his response.

**New Customers (Which Referral Strategy?):** This applies when you are testing different versions of the one type of referral strategy. For example, you may be running three different strategies over a three-week period. Give each one a code, and fill it in here.

**Details Captured:** Tick this column if you get the person's full name, address, and phone number. Just say, "I'd like to put you on our mailing list. Could I get your details, please?"

**Sales Conversion (Sale/Recruitment Made):** Tick this if the person buys something or decides to become a part of your network.

**Sales Conversion (Sale Value):** Write in the value of the sale.

**Sales Conversion (Follow Up/Call Back):** Tick this column if the customer does not buy and is to be followed up later. Alternately, tick this if the customer claims she will come back.

**Average Dollar Sale:** Divide the total takings for the day by the number of sales for the day. This will give you your average dollar sale.

**Conversion Rate Percent:** Divide the total number of customers that buy by the total number of customers and multiply the answer by 100. This will give you your conversion rate.

# Daily Testing & Measuring Sheet

**Name:** _____

**Date:** _____

| Inquiry # | Prospects Name | Repeat Customer | | New Customer | | | Details | Sales Conversion | | |
|---|---|---|---|---|---|---|---|---|---|---|
| | | New Inquiry | Same Inquiry | How Did They Hear About You | Which Marketing Strategy | Captured Y / N | | Sale Made | Sale Value | Follow Up/Call Back |
| 1 | | | | | | | | | | |
| 2 | | | | | | | | | | |
| 3 | | | | | | | | | | |
| 4 | | | | | | | | | | |
| 5 | | | | | | | | | | |
| 6 | | | | | | | | | | |
| 7 | | | | | | | | | | |
| 8 | | | | | | | | | | |
| 9 | | | | | | | | | | |
| 10 | | | | | | | | | | |
| 11 | | | | | | | | | | |
| 12 | | | | | | | | | | |
| 13 | | | | | | | | | | |
| TOTALS | | | | | | | | | | |

**AVG $$ SALE =** (Total of Sales Value column / Total No. of Sales Made)    _____ / _____ = _____

**CONVERSION RATE % =** (Total No. of Customers / Total No. of Sales Made)    _____ / _____ = _____

# ∎ Conclusion

So there you have it—21 powerful strategies on which to build a referral-based business. And the best part is that they have all been tried and tested and work remarkably well.

I have coached countless thousands of business all over the world over the years and I have encountered just about every type of challenge imaginable. There are also many common threads that run through most of them.

But perhaps the one thing I have learned through having worked with all these businesses is this: Your business really is much richer than you realize. You can easily find those hidden opportunities that will bring in extra profits. All you need to do is to apply what you have learned in this book and to read some of my other books.

All the additional profit you've been waiting to tap into will begin to flow as soon as you begin implementing these exciting strategies. Try them one at a time or in groups; the choice is yours. But whatever you do, don't do nothing, because then you'll continue getting the same results from your business that you're presently getting.

But if you want to see your business grow exponentially (and who doesn't?), it's time to get into *Action*.

# ▮ Getting into *Action*

## So, when is the best time to start?

*Now*—right now—so let me give you a step-by-step method to get yourself onto the same success path of many of my clients and the clients of my team at *Action International*.

Start testing and measuring now.

You'll want to ask your customers and prospects how they found out about you and your business. This will give you an idea of what's been working and what hasn't. You also want to concentrate on the five areas of the business chassis. Remember:

1. Number of Leads from each campaign.
2. Conversion Rate from each and every campaign.
3. Number of Transactions on average per year per customer.
4. Average Dollar Sale from each campaign.
5. Your Margins on each product or service.

The Number of Leads is easy; just take a measure for four weeks, average it out, and multiply by 50 working weeks of the year. Of course you'd ask each lead where they came from so you've got enough information to make advertising decisions.

The Conversion Rate is a little trickier, not because it's hard to measure, but because we want to know a few more details. You want to know what level of conversion you have from each and every type of marketing strategy you use. Remember that some customers won't buy right away, so keep accurate records on each and every lead.

To find the Number of Transactions you'll need to go through your records. Hopefully you can find the transaction history of at least 50 of your past customers and then average out their yearly purchases.

The Average Dollar Sale is as simple as it sounds. The total dollars sold divided by the number of sales. The best information you can collect is the average from each marketing campaign you run, so that you know where the real profit is coming from.

And, of course, your margins. An Average Margin is good to know and measure, but to know the margins on everything you sell is the most powerful knowledge you can collect.

If you're having any challenges with your testing and measuring, be sure to contact your nearest *Action International* Business Coach. She'll be able to help you through and show you the specialized documents to use.

If, by chance, you're thinking of racing ahead before you test and measure, remember this. It's impossible to improve a score when you don't know what the score is.

So you've got your starting point. You know exactly what's going on in your business right now. In fact, you know more about not only what's happening right now, but also the factors that are going to create what will happen tomorrow.

The next step in your business growth is simple.

Let's decide what you want out of the business—in other words, your goals. Here are the main points I want you to plan for.

How many hours do you want to work each week? How much money do you want to take out of the business each month? And, most importantly, when do you want to finish the business?

By "finish" the business, I mean when it will be systematized enough so it can run without your having to be there. Remember this about business; a little bit of planning goes a long way, but to make a plan you have to have a destination.

Once again, if you're having difficulty, talk to an *Action International* Business Coach. He'll know exactly how to help you find what it is you really want out of both your business and your life.

Now the real work begins.

Remember, our goal is to get a 10 percent increase in each area over the next 12 months. Choose well, but I want to warn you of one thing, one thing I can literally guarantee.

Eight out of 10 marketing campaigns you run *will not work.*

That's why when you choose to run, say, an advertising campaign in your local newspaper, you've got to run at least 10 different ads. When you select a direct mail campaign, you should send out at least 10 different letters to test, and so on.

Make sure you get at least five strategies under each heading and plan to run at least one, preferably two, at least each month for the next 12 months.

Don't work on just one of the five areas at a time; mix it up a little so you get the synergy of all five areas working together.

Now, this is the most important advice I can give you:

Learn how to make each and every strategy work. Don't just think you know what to do; go through my hints and tips, read more books, listen to as many tapes as you can, watch all the videos you can find, talk to the experts, and make sure you get the most advantage you can before you invest a whole lot of money.

The next 12 months are going to be a matter of doing the numbers, running the campaigns, testing headlines, testing offers, testing prices, and, of course, measuring the results.

By the end of it you should have at least five new strategies in each of the five areas working together to produce a great result.

Once again I want to stress that this will work and this will make your business grow as long as *you* work it.

Is it simple? *Yes.*

Is it easy? *No.*

You'll have to work hard. If you can get the guidance of someone who's been there before you, then get it.

Whatever you do, start it now, start it today, and most importantly, make the most of every day. Your past does not equal your future; you decide your future right here and right now.

## Getting into *Action*

*Be* who you want to be, *do* what you need to do, in order to *have* what you want to have.

Positive *thought* without positive *Action* leaves you with positively *nothing*. I called my company *Action International,* not Theory International, or Yeah, I read that book International, but *Action International.*

So take the first step—and get into *Action.*

# ■ ABOUT THE AUTHOR

## Bradley J. Sugars

Brad Sugars is a world-renowned Australian entrepreneur, author, and business coach who has helped more than a million clients around the world find business and personal success.

He's a trained accountant, but as he puts it, most of his experience comes from owning his own companies. Brad's been in business for himself since age 15 in some way or another, although his father would argue he started at 7 when he was caught selling his Christmas presents to his brothers. He's owned and operated more than two dozen companies, from pizza to ladies fashion, from real estate to insurance and many more.

His main company, *Action International*, started from humble beginnings in the back bedroom of a suburban home in 1993 when Brad started teaching business owners how to grow their sales and marketing results. Now *Action* has nearly 1000 franchises in 19 countries and is ranked in the top 100 franchises in the world.

Brad Sugars has spoken on stage with the likes of Tom Hopkins, Brian Tracy, John Maxwell, Robert Kiyosaki, and Allen Pease, written books with people like Anthony Robbins, Jim Rohn, and Mark Victor Hansen, appeared on countless TV and radio programs and in literally hundreds of print articles around the globe. He's been voted as one of the Most Admired Entrepreneurs by the readers of *E-Spy* magazine—next to the likes of Rupert Murdoch, Henry Ford, Richard Branson, and Anita Roddick.

Today, *Action International* has coaches across the globe and is ranked as one of the Top 25 Fastest Growing Franchises on the planet as well as the #1 Business Consulting Franchise. The success of *Action International* is simply attributed to the fact that they apply the strategies their coaches use with business owners.

Brad is a proud father and husband, the chairman of a major childrens' charity and in his own words, "a very average golfer."

Check out Brad's Web site www.bradsugars.com and read the literally hundreds of testimonials from those who've gone before you.

# ▌ RECOMMENDED READING LIST

## ACTION INTERNATIONAL BOOK LIST

"The only difference between *you* now and *you* in 5 years' time will be the people you meet and the books you read." Charlie Tremendous Jones

"And, the only difference between *your* income now and *your* income in 5 years' time will be the people you meet, the books you read, the tapes you listen to, and then how *you* apply it all." Brad Sugars

- *The E-Myth Revisited* by Michael E. Gerber
- *My Life in Advertising & Scientific Advertising* by Claude Hopkins
- *Tested Advertising Methods* by John Caples
- *Building the Happiness Centered Business* by Dr. Paddi Lund
- *Write Language* by Paul Dunn & Alan Pease
- *7 Habits of Highly Effective People* by Steven Covey
- *First Things First* by Steven Covey
- *Awaken the Giant Within* by Anthony Robbins
- *Unlimited Power* by Anthony Robbins
- *22 Immutable Laws of Marketing* by Al Ries & Jack Trout
- *21 Ways to Build a Referral Based Business* by Brad Sugars
- *21 Ways to Increase Your Advertising Response* by Mark Tier
- *The One Minute Salesperson* by Spencer Johnson & Larry Wilson
- *The One Minute Manager* by Spencer Johnson & Kenneth Blanchard
- *The Great Sales Book* by Jack Collis
- *Way of the Peaceful Warrior* by Dan Millman
- *How to Build a Championship Team*—Six Audio tapes by Blair Singer
- Brad Sugars "Introduction to Sales & Marketing" 3-hour Video
- Leverage—Board Game by Brad Sugars
- *17 Ways to Increase Your Business Profits* booklet & tape by Brad Sugars. FREE OF CHARGE to Business Owners

**\*To order Brad Sugars' products from the recommended reading list, call your nearest *Action International* office today.**

# The 18 Most Asked Questions about Working with an *Action International* Business Coach

## And 18 great reasons why you'll jump at the chance to get your business flying and make your dreams come true

### 1. So who is *Action International?*

*Action International* is a business Coaching and Consulting company started in 1993 by entrepreneur and author Brad Sugars. With offices around the globe and business coaches from Singapore to Sydney to San Francisco, *Action International* has been set up with you, the business owner, in mind.

Unlike traditional consulting firms, *Action* is designed to give you both short-term assistance and long-term training through its affordable Mentoring approach. After 12 years teaching business owners how to succeed, *Action's* more than 10,000 clients and 1,000,000 seminar attendees will attest to the power of the programs.

Based on the sales, marketing, and business management systems created by Brad Sugars, your *Action* Coach is trained to not only show you how to increase your business revenues and profits, but also how to develop the business so that you as the owner work less and relax more.

*Action International* is a franchised company, so your local *Action* Coach is a fellow business owner who's invested her own time, money, and energy to make her business succeed. At *Action,* your success truly does determine our success.

### 2. And, why do I need a Business Coach?

Every great sports star, business person, and superstar is surrounded by coaches and advisors.

And, as the world of business moves faster and gets more competitive, it's difficult to keep up with both the changes in your industry and the innovations in sales, marketing, and management strategies. Having a business coach is no longer a luxury; it's become a necessity.

On top of all that, it's impossible to get an objective answer from yourself. Don't get me wrong. You can survive in business without the help of a Coach, but it's almost impossible to thrive.

A Coach *can* see the forest for the trees. A Coach will make you focus on the game. A Coach will make you run more laps than you feel like. A Coach will tell it like it is. A Coach will give you small pointers. A Coach will listen. A Coach will be your marketing manager, your sales director, your training coordinator, your partner, your confidant, your mentor, your best friend, and an *Action* Business Coach will help you make your dreams come true.

### 3. Then, what's an Alignment Consultation?

Great question. It's where an *Action* Coach starts with every business owner. You'll invest a minimum of $1295, and during the initial 2 to 3 hours your Coach invests with you, he'll learn as much as he can about your business, your goals, your challenges, your sales, your marketing, your finances, and so much more.

All with three goals in mind: To know exactly where your business is now. To clarify your goals both in the business and personally. And thirdly, to get the crucial pieces of information he needs to create your businesses *Action* Plan for the next 12 months.

Not a traditional business or marketing plan mind you, but a step-by-step plan of *Action* that you'll work through as you continue with the Mentor Program.

### 4. So, what, then, is the Mentor Program?

Simply put, it's where your *Action* Coach will work with you for a full 12 months to make your goals a reality. From weekly coaching calls and goal-setting sessions, to creating marketing pieces together, you will develop new sales strategies and business systems so you can work less and learn all that you need to know about how to make your dreams come true.

You'll invest between $995 and $10,000 a month and your Coach will dedicate a minimum of 5 hours a month to working with you on your sales, marketing, team building, business development, and every step of the *Action* Plan you created from your Alignment Consultation.

Unlike most consultants, your *Action* Coach will do more than just show you what to do. She'll be with you when you need her most, as each idea takes shape, as each campaign is put into place, as you need the little pointers on making it happen, when you need someone to talk to, when you're faced with challenges and, most importantly, when you're just not sure what to do next. Your Coach will be there every step of the way.

### 5. Why at least 12 months?

~~If you've been in business for more than a few weeks, you've seen at least one~~ or two so called "quick fixes."

Most Consultants seem to think they can solve all your problems in a few hours or a few days. At *Action* we believe that long-term success means not just scraping the surface and doing it for you. It means doing it with you, showing you how to do it, working alongside you, and creating the success together.

Over the 12 months, you'll work on different areas of your business, and month by month you'll not only see your goals become a reality, you'll gain both the confidence and the knowledge to make it happen again and again, even when your first 12 months of Coaching is over.

### 6. How can you be sure this will work in my industry and in my business?

Very simple. You see at *Action,* we're experts in the areas of sales, marketing, business development, business management, and team building just to name a few. With 328 different profit-building strategies, you'll soon see just how powerful these systems are.

*You,* on the other hand, are the expert in your business and together we can apply the *Action* systems to make your business fly.

Add to this the fact that within the *Action* Team at least one of our Coaches has either worked with, managed, worked in, or even owned a business that's the same or very similar to yours. Your *Action* Coach has the full resources of the entire *Action* team to call upon for every challenge you have. Imagine hundreds of experts ready to help you.

### 7. Won't this just mean more work?

Of course when you set the plan with your *Action* Coach, it'll all seem like a massive amount of work, but no one ever said attaining your goals would be easy.

In the first few months, it'll take some work to adjust, some work to get over the hump so to speak. The further you are into the program, the less and less work you'll have to do.

You will, however, be literally amazed at how focused you'll be and how much you'll get done. With focus, an *Action* Coach, and most importantly the *Action* Systems, you'll be achieving a whole lot more with the same or even less work.

### 8. How will I find the time?

Once again the first few months will be the toughest, not because of an extra amount of work, but because of the different work. In fact, your *Action* Coach will show you how to, on a day-to-day basis, get more work done with less effort.

In other words, after the first few months you'll find that you're not working more, just working differently. Then, depending on your goals from about month six onwards, you'll start to see the results of all your work, and if you choose to, you can start working less than ever before. Just remember, it's about changing what you do with your time, *not* putting in more time.

### 9. How much will I need to invest?

Nothing, if you look at it from the same perspective as we do. That's the difference between a cost and an investment. Everything you do with your *Action* Coach is a true investment in your future.

Not only will you create great results in your business, but you'll end up with both an entrepreneurial education second to none, and the knowledge that you can repeat your successes over and over again.

As mentioned, you'll need to invest at least $1295 up to $5000 for the Alignment Consultation and Training Day, and then between $995 and $10,000 a month for the next 12 months of coaching.

Your Coach may also suggest several books, tapes, and videos to assist in your training, and yes, they'll add to your investment as you go. Why? Because having an *Action* Coach is just like having a marketing manager, a sales team leader, a trainer, a recruitment specialist, and corporate consultant all for half the price of a secretary.

### 10. Will it cost me extra to implement the strategies?

Once again, give your *Action* Coach just half an hour and he'll show you how to turn your marketing into an investment that yields sales and profits rather than just running up your expenses.

In most cases we'll actually save you money when we find the areas that aren't working for you. But yes, I'm sure you'll need to spend some money to make some money.

Yet, when you follow our simple testing and measuring systems, you'll never risk more than a few dollars on each campaign, and when we find the ones that work, we make sure you keep profiting from them time and again.

Remember, when you go the accounting way of saving costs, you can only ever add a few percent to the bottom line.

Following Brad Sugars' formula, your *Action* Coach will show you that through sales, marketing, and income growth, your possible returns are exponential.

The sky's the limit, as they say.

### 11. Are there any guarantees?

To put it bluntly, no. Your *Action* Coach will never promise any specific results, nor will she guarantee that any of your goals will become a reality.

You see, we're your coach. You're still the player, and it's up to you to take the field. Your Coach will push you, cajole you, help you, be there for you, and even do some things with you, but you've still got to do the work.

Only *you* can ever be truly accountable for your own success and at *Action* we know this to be a fact. We guarantee to give you the best service we can, to answer your questions promptly, and with the best available information. And, last but not least your *Action* Coach is committed to making you successful whether you like it or not.

That's right, once we've set the goals and made the plan, we'll do whatever it takes to make sure you reach for that goal and strive with all your might to achieve all that you desire.

Of course we'll be sure to keep you as balanced in your life as we can. We'll make sure you never compromise either the long-term health and success of your company or yourself, and more importantly your personal set of values and what's important to you.

### 12. What results have other business owners seen?

Anything from previously working 60 hours a week down to working just 10—right through to increases in revenues of 100s and even 1000s of percent. Results speak for themselves. Be sure to keep reading for specific examples of real people, with real businesses, getting real results.

There are three reasons why this will work for you in your business. Firstly, your *Action* Coach will help you get 100 percent focused on your goals and the step-by-step processes to get you there. This focus alone is amazing in its effect on you and your business results.

Secondly, your coach will hold you accountable to get things done, not just for the day-to-day running of the business, but for the dynamic growth of the business. You're investing in your success and we're going to get you there.

Thirdly, your Coach is going to teach you one-on-one as many of *Action's* 328 profit-building strategies as you need. So whether your goal is to be making more money, or working fewer hours or both inside the next 12 months your goals can become a reality. Just ask any of the thousands of existing *Action* clients, or more specifically, check out the results of 19 of our most recent clients shown later in this section.

### 13. What areas will you coach me in?

There are five main areas your *Action* Coach will work on with you. Of course, how much of each depends on you, your business, and your goals.

Sales. The backbone of creating a superprofitable business, and one area we'll help you get spectacular results in.

Marketing and Advertising. If you want to get a sale, you've got to get a prospect. Over the next 12 months your *Action* Coach will teach you Brad Sugars' amazingly simple streetwise marketing—marketing that makes profits.

Team Building and Recruitment. You'll never *wish* for the right people again. You'll have motivated and passionate team members when your Coach shows you how.

Systems and Business Development. Stop the business from running you and start running your business. Your Coach will show you the secrets to having the business work, even when you're not there.

Customer Service. How to deliver consistently, make it easy to buy, and leave your customers feeling delighted with your service. Both referrals and repeat business are centered in the strategies your Coach will teach you.

### 14. Can you also train my people?

Yes. We believe that training your people is almost as important as coaching you.

Your investment starts at $1500 for your entire team, and you can decide between five very powerful in-house training programs. From "*Sales Made Simple*" for your face-to-face sales team to "*Phone Power*" for your entire team's telephone etiquette and sales ability. Then you can run the *"Raving Fans"* customer service training or the *"Total Team"* training. And finally, if you're too busy earning a living to make any real money, then you've just got to attend our *"Business Academy 101."* It will make a huge impact on your finances, business, career, family, and lifestyle. You'll be amazed at how much involvement and excitement comes out of your team with each training program.

### 15. Can you write ads, letters, and marketing pieces for me?

Yes. Your *Action* Coach can do it for you, he can train you to do it yourself, or we can simply critique the marketing pieces you're using right now.

If you want us to do it for you, our one-time fees start at just $1195. You'll not only get one piece; we'll design several pieces for you to take to the market and see which one performs the best. Then, if it's a critique you're after, just $349 means we'll work through your entire piece and give you feedback on what to change, how to change it, and what else you should do. Last but not least, for between $15 and $795 we can recommend a variety of books, tapes, and most importantly, Brad Sugars' Instant Success series books that'll take you step-by-step through the how-tos of creating your marketing pieces.

### 16. Why do you also recommend books, tapes, and videos?

Basically, to save you time and money. Take Brad Sugars' *Sales Rich* DVD or Video Series, for instance. In about 16 hours you'll learn more about business than you have in the last 12 years. It'll also mean your *Action* Coach works with you on the high-level implementation rather than the very basic teaching.

It's a very powerful way for you to speed up the coaching process and get phenomenal rather than just great results.

### 17. When is the best time to get started?

Yesterday. OK, seriously, right now, today, this minute, before you take another step, waste another dollar, lose another sale, work too many more hours, miss another family event, forget another special occasion.

Far too many business people wait and see. They think working harder will make it all better. Remember, what you know got you to where you are. To get to where you want to go, you've got to make some changes and most probably learn something new.

There's no time like the present to get started on your dreams and goals.

### 18. So how do we get started?

Well, you'd better get back in touch with your *Action* Coach. There's some very simple paperwork to sign, and then you're on your way.

You'll have to invest a few hours showing them everything about your business. Together you'll get a plan created and then the work starts. Remember, it may seem like a big job at the start, but with a Coach, you're sharing the load and together you'll achieve great things.

# Here's what others say about what happened after working with an *Action* business coach

### Paul and Rosemary Rose—Icontact Multimedia

"Our *Action* coach showed us several ways to help market our product. We went on to triple our client base and simultaneously tripled our profits in just seven months. It was unbelievable! Last year was our best Christmas ever. We were really able to spoil ourselves!"

### S. Ford—Pride Kitchens

"In 6 months, I've gone from working more than 60 hours per week in my business to less than 20, and my conversion rate's up from 19 percent to 62 percent. I've now got some life back!"

### Gary and Leanne Paper—Galea Timber Products

"We achieved our goal for the 12 months within a 6-month period with a 100 percent increase in turnover and a good increase in margins. We have already recommended and will continue to recommend this program to others."

### Russell, Kevin, John, and Karen—Northern Lights Power and Distribution

"Our profit margin has increased from 8 percent to 21 percent in the last 8 months. *Action* coaching focussed us on what are our most profitable markets."

### Ty Pedersen—De Vries Marketing Sydney

"After just three months of coaching, my sales team's conversion rate has grown from an average of less than 12 percent to more than 23 percent and our profits have climbed by more than 30 percent."

### Hank Meerkerk and Hemi McGarvey—B.O.P. School of Welding

"Last year we started off with a profit forecast, but as soon as we got *Action* involved we decided to double our forecast. We're already well over that forecast again by two-and-a-half times on turnover, and profits are even higher. Now we run a really profitable business."

### Stuart Birch—Education Personnel Limited

"One direct mail letter added $40,000 to my bottom line, and working with *Action* has given me quality time to work on my business and spend time with my family."

### Mark West—Wests Pumping and Irrigation

"In four months two simple strategies have increased our business more than 20 percent. We're so busy, we've had to delay expanding the business while we catch up!"

### Michael Griffiths—Gym Owner

"I went from working 70 hours per week *in* the business to just 25 hours, with the rest of the time spent working *on* the business."

### Cheryl Standring—In Harmony Landscapes

"We tried our own direct mail and only got a 1 percent response. With *Action* our response rate increased to 20 percent. It's definitely worth every dollar we've invested."

### Jason and Chris Houston—Empradoor Finishing

"After 11 months of working with *Action,* we have increased our sales by 497 percent, and the team is working without our having to be there."

### Michael Avery—Coomera Pet Motels

"I was skeptical at first, but I knew we needed major changes in our business. In 2 months, our extra profits were easily covering our investment and our predictions for the next 10 months are amazing."

### Garry Norris—North Tax & Accounting

"As an accountant, my training enables me to help other business people make more money. It is therefore refreshing when someone else can help me do the same. I have a policy of only referring my clients to people who are professional, good at what they do, and who have personally given me great service. *Action* fits all three of these criteria, and I recommend *Action* to my business clients who want to grow and develop their businesses further."

### Lisa Davis and Steve Groves—Mt. Eden Motorcycles

"With *Action* we increased our database from 800 to 1200 in 3 months. We consistently get about 20 new qualified people on our database each week for less than $10 per week."

### Christine Pryor—U-Name-It Embroidery

"Sales for August this year have increased 352 percent. We're now targeting a different market and we're a lot more confident about what we're doing."

### Joseph Saitta and Michelle Fisher—Banyule Electrics

"Working with *Action*, our inquiry rate has doubled. In four months our business has changed so much our customers love us. It's a better place for people to work and our margins are widening."

### Kevin and Alison Snook—Property Sales

"In the 12 months previous to working with *Action*, we had sold one home in our subdivision. In the first eight months of working with *Action*, we sold six homes. The results speak for themselves."

### Wayne Manson—Hospital Supplies

"When I first looked at the Mentoring Program it looked expensive, but from the inside looking out, its been the best money I have ever spent. Sales are up more than $3000 per month since I started, and the things I have learned and expect to learn will ensure that I will enjoy strong sustainable growth in the future."

# ■ *Action* Contact Details

***Action International* Asia Pacific**

Ground Floor, *Action* House, 2 Mayneview Street, Milton QLD 4064

Ph: +61 (0) 7 3368 2525

Fax: +61 (0) 7 3368 2535

Free Call: 1800 670 335

***Action International* Europe**

Olympic House, Harbor Road, Howth, Co. Dublin, Ireland

Ph: +353 (0) 1-8320213

Fax: +353 (0) 1-8394934

***Action International* North America**

5670 Wynn Road Suite A & C, Las Vegas, Nevada 89118

Ph: +1 (702) 795 3188

Fax: +1 (702) 795 3183

Free Call: (888) 483 2828

***Action International* UK**

3-5 Richmond Hill, Richmond, Surrey, TW 106RE

Ph: +44 020 8948 5151

Fax: +44 020 8948 4111

*Action* Offices around the globe:

Australia | Canada | China | England | France | Germany | Hong Kong

India | Indonesia | Ireland | Malaysia | Mexico | New Zealand

Phillippines | Scotland | Spain | Singapore | USA | Wales

## Here's how you can profit from all of Brad's ideas with your local *Action* International **Business Coach**

Just like a sporting coach pushes an athlete to achieve optimum performance, provides them with support when they are exhausted, and teaches the athlete to execute plays that the competition does not anticipate.

A business coach will make you run more laps than you feel like. A business coach will show it like it is. And a business coach will listen.

The role of an *Action* Business Coach is to show you how to improve your business through guidance, support, and encouragement. Your coach will help you with your sales, marketing, management, team building, and so much more. Just like a sporting coach, your *Action* Business Coach will help you and your business perform at levels you never thought possible.

Whether you've been in business for a week or 20 years, it's the right time to meet with and see how you'll profit from an *Action* Coach.

As the owner of a business it's hard enough to keep pace with all the changes and innovations going on in your industry, let alone to find the time to devote to sales, marketing, systems, planning and team management, and then to run your business as well.

As the world of business moves faster and becomes more competitive, having a Business Coach is no longer a luxury; it has become a necessity. Based on the sales, marketing, and business management systems created by Brad Sugars, your *Action* Coach is trained to not only show you how to increase your business revenues and profits but also how to develop your business so that you, as the owner, can take back control. All with the aim of your working less and relaxing more. Making money is one thing; having the time to enjoy it is another.

Your *Action* Business Coach will become your marketing manager, your sales director, your training coordinator, your confidant, your mentor. In short, your *Action* Coach will help you make your business dreams come true.

## ATTENTION BUSINESS OWNERS
### You can increase your profits now

Here's how you can have one of Brad's *Action* International Business Coaches guide you to success.

Like every successful sporting icon or team, a business needs a coach to help it achieve its full potential. In order to guarantee your business success, you can have one of Brad's team as your business coach. You will learn about how you can get amazing results with the help of the team at *Action* International.

The business coaches are ready to take you and your business on a journey that will reward you for the rest of your life. You see, we believe *Action* speaks louder than words.

Complete and post this card to your local *Action* office to discover how our team can help you increase your income today!

*Action* International

### The World's Number-1 Business Coaching Team

Name ........................................................................................................................................

Position ....................................................................................................................................

Company ..................................................................................................................................

Address ....................................................................................................................................

.................................................................................................................................................

Country ....................................................................................................................................

Phone .......................................................................................................................................

Fax ...........................................................................................................................................

Email ........................................................................................................................................

Referred by ..............................................................................................................................

# How do I become an *Action* International **Business Coach?**

If you choose to invest your time and money in a great business and you're looking for a white-collar franchise opportunity to build yourself a lifestyle, an income, a way to take control of your life and, a way to get great personal satisfaction …

**Then you've just found the world's best team!**

Now, it's about finding out if you've got what it takes to really enjoy and thrive in this amazing business opportunity.

**Here are the 4 things we look for in every *Action* Coach:**

**1. You've got to love succeeding**

We're looking for people who love success, who love getting out there and making things happen. People who enjoy mixing with other people, people who thrive on learning and growing, and people who want to charge an hourly rate most professionals only dream of.

**2. You've got to love being in charge of your own life**

When you're ready to take control, the key is to be in business for yourself, but not by yourself. ***Action***'s support, our training, our world leading systems, and the backup of a global team are all waiting to give you the best chance of being an amazing business success.

**3. You've got to love helping people**

Being a great Coach is all about helping yourself by helping others. The first time clients thank you for showing them step by step how to make more money and work less within their business, will be the day you realize just how great being an ***Action*** Business Coach really is.

**4. You've got to love a great lifestyle**

Working from home, setting your own timetable, spending time with family and friends, knowing that the hard work you do is for your own company and, not having to climb a so-called corporate ladder. This is what lifestyle is all about. Remember, business is supposed to give you a life, not take it away.

Our business is booming and we're seriously looking for people ready to find out more about how becoming a member of the ***Action*** International Business Coaching team is going to be the best decision you've ever made.

**Apply online now at www.action-international.com**

**Here's how you can network, get new leads, build yourself an instant sales team, learn, grow and build a great team of supportive business owners around you by checking into your local *Action* Profit Club**

**Joining your local *Action* Profit Club is about more than just networking, it's also the learning and exchanging of profitable ideas.**

Embark on a journey to a more profitable enterprise by meeting with fellow, like-minded business owners.

An *Action* Profit Club is an excellent way to network with business people and business owners. You will meet every two weeks for breakfast to network and learn profitable strategies to grow your business.

Here are three reasons why *Action* *International's* Profit Clubs work where other networking groups don't:

1.  You know networking is a great idea. The challenge is finding the time and maintaining the motivation to keep it up and make it a part of your business. If you're not really having fun and getting the benefits, you'll find it gets easier to find excuses that stop you going. So, we guarantee you will always have fun and learn a lot from your bi-weekly group meetings.
2.  The real problem is that so few people do any work 'on' their business. Instead they generally work "in" it, until it's too late. By being a member of an *Action* Profit Club, you get to attend FREE business-building workshops run by Business Coaches that teach you how to work "on" your business and avoid this common pitfall and help you to grow your business.
3.  Unlike other groups, we have marketing systems to assist in your groups' growth rather than just relying on you to bring in new members. This way you can concentrate on YOUR business rather than on ours.

Latest statistics show that the average person knows at least 200 other contacts. By being a member of your local *Action* Profit Club, you have an instant network of around 3,000 people

**Join your local *Action* Profit Club today.**

**Apply online now at www.actionprofitclub.com**

## LEVERAGE—The Game of Business
## Your Business Success is just a Few Games Away

Leverage—The Game of Business is a fun way to learn how to succeed in business fast.

**The rewards start flowing the moment you start playing!**

Leverage is three hours of fun, learning, and discovering how you can be an amazingly successful business person.

It's a breakthrough in education that will have you racking up the profits in no time. The principles you take away from playing this game will set you up for a life of business success. It will open your mind to what's truly possible. Apply what you learn and **sit back and watch your profits soar.**

By playing this fun and interactive business game, you will learn:

- How to quickly raise your business income
- How business people can become rich and successful in a short space of time
- How to create a business that works without you

**Isn't it time you had the edge over your competition?**

Leverage has been played by all age groups from 12-85 and has been a huge learning experience for all. The most common comment we hear is: 'I thought I knew a lot, and just by playing a simple board game I have realized I have a long way to go. The knowledge I've gained from playing Leverage will make me thousands! Thanks for the lesson.'

**To order your copy online today, please visit www.bradsugars.com**

# *Instant Success* series.

**INSTANT CASHFLOW**
Turn every lead into a sale
(0-07-146659-2)

**BILLIONAIRE IN TRAINING**
Learn the wealth building secrets
of billionaires
(0-07-146661-4)

**INSTANT PROFIT**
Boost your bottom line with
a cash-building plan
(0-07-146668-1)

**SUCCESSFUL FRANCHISING**
Learn how to buy or sell a franchise
(0-07-146671-1)

**INSTANT ADVERTISING**
Create ads that stand out and sell
(0-07-146660-6)

**INSTANT REFERRALS**
Never cold call or chase after
customers again
(0-07-146667-3)

**INSTANT LEADS**
Generate a steady flow of leads
(0-07-146663-0)

**INSTANT SYSTEMS**
Stop running your business and start
growing it
(0-07-146670-3)

**INSTANT TEAM BUILDING**
Learn the six keys to a winning team
(0-07-146669-X)

*Your source for the strategies, skills,
and confidence every business owner
needs to succeed.*